Fostering Love and Laughter:

A Slightly Exaggerated Memoir About My Life in Animal Rescue

By

Sunshine Richards

Thank you to the Bedford Humane Society in Bedford, Virginia for
allowing me to collect and share the stories contained in this
book. It has been one of the greatest honors of my life to be part
of this important work.

Dedication

To my boys and my parents who have gone on this journey with me, bottle-feeding, responding to midnight cries with cuddles, scrubbing poo out of carpets, and putting in countless hours building a space for more furbabies. And to my rescue friends and those I don't yet know that work tirelessly in the world of animal rescue. It is ugly, messy, draining work that carries with it a reward like no other.

TABLE OF CONTENTS

1 SHE CAN'T HELP IT SHE SMELLS LIKE PEE

You know how sometimes you're out at the store and you suddenly smell pee? And so you start casually glancing around you to see where it's coming from, expecting to see a grungy little toddler or, at the very least, a disheveled old man shuffling down the aisle … except you don't see any of those. And then maybe you start scanning the aisle floor for puddles … but nope. And so you start to pick up the cereal box in front of you to give it a whiff and then you realize that the smell is actually coming from you?

… No?

Really? Huh. Ok. So, apparently you haven't spent any length of time in animal rescue (or child care … but I haven't spent a whole lot of time in that area, either. Except my own children's. I cared for my own children. Which I think probably does make me an expert, but even so, that's not what this book is about.). So, I'm going to spend the next 50 or 100 or 500 pages giving you some insights into just what it's like to work and volunteer in animal rescue. I'm not real clear on exactly how many pages we're looking at here 'cause I'm kind of writing as I go, putting the experiences to paper as they happen. I suppose I could go back later, when the book is done, and edit this part for accuracy. But if you know me, you recognize how wildly ridiculous that idea is. I'm not even sure why you'd suggest it. Forever forward, I say, except when I've inadvertently passed the coffee aisle. I'm definitely backing up to hit the coffee aisle.

So, what this is, is a collection of true stories from my animal fostering experiences. These things actually happened. I know some of you are going to say, "Dude, animals can't talk." To you I say, stop being such a buzzkill, and also, yes they can. Because when I'm having one of my especially emotional crazy hormonal moods where

I'm sobbing hysterically at the Hallmark commercial on the television, my dog is absolutely mumbling in judgement as he lumbers out of the room to get some peace in his study. (He calls it his study. It's not his. It's mine. But I let him call it his in hopes that he might get industrious and maybe use it to start his own business and actually start contributing a little bit around here.)

But if you've spent any time in animal rescue, you know that animals absolutely talk. If you just pay enough attention to their eyes, their tails, their really sharp claws, you'll hear what they're saying to you. It just so happens that I hear the actual words.

And tone. Oh, they've got a tone. Those little calico cats have all kinds of tone.

So here are the stories of just a few of the dogs and cats that I've had the privilege to foster through a small local humane society here in Southwest Virginia. Some of them have devastating stories to share, some have a wonderful sense of humor, and some have attitude. So much attitude. I mentioned the tone, right? Freakin' calicos, man. So much damn tone.

Maybe these stories will encourage you to support your local rescue. Maybe they will push you to foster or adopt. (Sometimes those are the same thing, but we'll get back to that later.) If nothing else, I hope this book will help you not judge the poor, exhausted chick at the grocery store who happens to smell like cat pee, which is really the worst kind of pee, because she's doing the best she can, dammit.

2 TALKING BABY TALK TO MY COUCH

This is awkward. Damn, I'm getting too old for this mess. The tile floor felt cold against my bare legs as I lay there straining to see under the blue plaid couch. I was sure he was under there. I had already checked under the other furniture, and I had been very clear with my sons that no one besides me could come down to the basement. He couldn't have gotten out. He was just hiding. I was sure of it. I looked behind the books on the built-in bookshelves. I looked behind the television. I pulled the crate out and checked behind it. I had admittedly even lifted it up to look underneath. I can't explain why I had taken that step before looking under the furniture. I was a little panicked, and I was prepared for the most horrific outcome. I crawled around on the floor looking under chairs and loveseats. Why do we have so many freaking loveseats?! Nothing. I belly-crawled my way to the plaid couch. He must be under this one. Initially, the cold floor felt refreshing on such a hot day, but after laying there for thirty minutes, I was beginning to get chilled.

And impatient.

"AppleJaaaaack. Sweet, sweet AppleJaaaaack."

I was using the softest, sweetest, baby voice I had, but all I got in return was silence. I cautiously slipped my hand further under the couch anticipating vicious teeth latching on, possibly striking a vein.

A trip to the ER.

Futile attempts to wash blood stains off the wall.

"Little AJ JackJack. You can come out sweet handsome boy. You're safe here, sweet AppleJackie JackJack."

When I could see no sign of orange fur under the couch, I cautiously ran my hand along the underside and felt a lump. I held my hand there for a moment to see if the lump would move. I was sure this was no ordinary lump, and I was determined to wait him out until he proved me right. Admittedly, my confidence began to waiver after ten solid minutes of waiting. My shoulder began to ache from holding my arm at an odd angle maintaining contact with the lump. Everything was silent. I don't even think I was breathing. Finally, I felt the lump shift slightly.

"Applejackie! AJ Jackie Jack Jack! You're here! You should come out and see me little boy." I wonder how comforting it is to have some obviously mentally unstable woman blocking your only means of escape and calling you what is clearly not your name. His response told me that it was definitely not comforting.

"Lady, the name is APPLEJACK. Really, it's not that hard. And I'm gonna advise you to remove your hand from my safe space. Now." I could hear him and I didn't want to provoke him. I just wanted to see his beautiful little face and tell him he would be ok. I wanted to cuddle him. His fluffy orange fur looked awfully cuddly.

"Why did you let him out of the crate?" Mindy would ask me later.

"Ummmmmm, cause he told me he wanted out?"

"Really? The cat told you he wanted out? You're a special kind of special, aren't you?"

She was probably right. I'd brought this gorgeous orange long-haired cat with the big greens eyes home three days ago after his original adopter returned him to us for reasons I couldn't quite understand. I set up a large dog crate and filled it with everything he would need to feel comfortable. I draped a large sheet over it to help him feel secure. I'd fed him and cleaned his litter box and almost petted him once. Still, he would sit there, eyes cast downward, cowering behind his litter box. For three days I tried to coax him into trusting me, but he remained silent and unmoving.

I needed a different approach. Maybe he was feeling trapped in the crate. If I let him out of the crate, he could explore the basement area in peace and start to feel more relaxed. I, in all my genius, thought that having access to a more wide open space might make him feel more secure. I opened his crate, told him he could come out and play, then left him alone to explore. I thought that when I returned to the basement later that night, Applejack would be so grateful to me for freeing him, he would immediately run to me, throw his front paws around my leg, and express his love and adoration for me. Instead, he disappeared. He disappeared into my couch. Not under it, mind you, but actually IN it. He found a hole in the bottom lining and climbed up inside. There was evidence that he would come out of the couch to eat or use the litter box, but never when I was present. He wanted nothing to do with me and all the baby talk in the world wasn't going to change his mind.

So here I was lying on my cold basement floor, freezing, hand tentatively stretched under the couch, talking baby talk to, well, to my couch. It wasn't working, and I was feeling like an utter foster failure. And I couldn't remember the last time I'd actually cleaned the floor. I definitely couldn't remember ever cleaning under the couch where my hand was currently resting gingerly upon something not quite sticky but not quite solid, either. This is my life now. Three years with the local humane society had brought me to this point.

Working from home allowed me to devote much of my time to animal rescue. When people ask me what I do for a living, I tell them I'm a criminal justice instructor. In truth, I'm more of a glorified cat maid. I spend a large portion of my day filling food dishes, scooping poo out of boxes, and wiping vomit and hairballs up off of the most random of places throughout my house. Seriously, inside of a rolled up yoga mat in the closet? But how…?

I'd seen the humane society newsletter asking for families to help foster animals. Before that moment, I hadn't even realized such a thing as animal fostering existed. This sounded like something I must do. My two teenage sons were excited when I told them about this decision. I, too, was excited and eager to get started. What better way to volunteer my time and give back to my community than to spend my free time playing with puppies and cuddling with kittens?

The reality of animal fostering isn't quite so glamorous. When I decided to start fostering, scrubbing poo out of my bedroom rug wasn't exactly what I had envisioned. The playing and cuddling is what I was focused on. I was certain that there would be a lot of playing and a lot of cuddling.

I was also going to start working part-time as the office manager for the humane society, so that was just going to be bonus puppy and kitten cuddles and totally not heartbreak, anger, and frustration. Honestly, the reality of animal rescue is equal parts awesome and devastation. It allows you to see the best humans the world has to offer and also the absolute worst. It generates your deepest wells of love and your most homicidal urges. And it is all so completely worth it.

Before we started fostering we had one pet. We had adopted Lobo three years earlier from another humane society. He was an eight-week old Rottweiler/English Setter mix that had grown into ninety pounds of fur and sweetness and joy by the time we brought home our first foster animals. Little did I know how drastically the decision to foster animals would change all of our lives.

I started my fostering career with a tiny little kitten I named Gracie. She was a stray that the board president had found and brought to the humane society office to be the office cat. She was only supposed to stay with me over the weekend because there were no other foster homes available to take her, and I didn't want to leave her in the humane society office alone for two days. However, as soon as I brought her into my home, I knew she could never leave. I called the board president to tell her I wanted to adopt Gracie.

"Oh, I knew that days ago."

"You did? Cause I didn't know until just now. How could you know before I knew?"

"It was obvious. Just wait. She won't be your last."

Foster failure number one. That was a quick one. And so it begins.

3 ALWAYS KEEP TISSUES IN YOUR CAR

You ever visit your local pound? Nah, probably not. I mean, it's not like some hangout joint or a place to pick up dudes. Or chicks. Or, I mean, sometimes there are chicks. Rabbits. Ferrets. Ours had a pig once. Even two wolf-dog hybrids. But they won't let you pet those. Or adopt them. But if you're in animal rescue, or perhaps if you've ever adopted a pet, you've possibly visited a pound or two.

Something happens to most people when they walk through their local pound. Traditionally, they're not exactly happy places. They're sad. Like, gut-wrenching, soul-crushing, ugly cry in front of the world kind of sad. These are places of overwhelming sadness, especially for those of us that see the depth of love and purity of soul in the eyes of our pets. We know the great range of emotion they are capable of experiencing and the unconditional acceptance and love they are capable of giving. So, I wasn't really prepared for what I was about to experience my first time going in. I was all, "here I go to save a dog" (sung in the Underdog voice … or was it Mighty Mouse … whatever, you know what I mean. Just sing it.).

When I walk through the pound now, I see dogs that react to their situation in one of three ways. Some dogs appear to remain positively aloof to the fate they face. They bounce around in their kennel, wagging their tails and smiling happily at any human that walks past. Complete goofballs. It's tragically adorable. They are not actually aloof, though. They are demonstrating a very cunning survival mechanism. They are fully aware that adoption or rescue is their only chance for survival and so they make every attempt they can to draw the attention of that one person that might save their life. I've fostered a few of those.

Some dogs get aggressive, growling and barking, daring someone to come into their kennel and try something. And by

13

someone, I mean me. It's me they're daring. Because I fully believe I have a vicious dog rehabilitation super power. In my defense, there's precedent. Just keep reading. You'll see. These are the dogs most likely to be euthanized quickly, seemingly vicious and dangerous and unadoptable. They are quickly passed over by the few families that come through looking for a new pet. Most people don't want to risk their new pet biting little Bobby's face off, even if little Bobby is kind of bratty and could use some real discipline. The thing is, most of these dogs are not actually vicious at all. It's all an act. They are terrified and demonstrating a less successful survival mechanism than the goofy showman dogs. It's understandable, really. They know what this place is, what happens here. They see it. They see it because, quite tragically, animals are often euthanized right there in front of the others. Seriously. In many pounds today, animals are killed right in front of the other animals. Like, what in the actual world? Right? Can you imagine the reaction of human rights activists if we put humans to death that way? (I know some of you are reading this thinking, hey, that's actually a great idea! Maybe. But that's not what this book is about.)

Now, let me say that my local pound has gone through some major changes, and the staff and volunteers in there today are phenomenal. But there was a time, and much of it during the writing of this book, when that was not the case. Because county pounds can really attract a low quality of being. Like, psychopath/sociopath level. (I'm throwing both in here because I've never really had a strong grasp on the difference and since that's not the actual focus of this book, I'm unmotivated to do any research on it.) (But I think it's probably sociopath that I'm looking for here. Yeah, definitely sociopath. I feel pretty confident about that.) (But clearly not confident enough to go back and edit it, so I'm going to leave both in.)

These aggressive dogs are not only overlooked by potential adopters, but rescues are reluctant to pull them out of the pound, as well. They represent a significant liability if they are adopted out and then bite someone. There is also the risk that they won't be adopted at all and then what do you do with them? So, most of them remain in the pound until their death. Occasionally, though, some make it out, and the immediate change in demeanor once they realize they are finally in a safe place is nothing short of miraculous. I've fostered a few of those.

The third type of dog has simply given up. Immediately upon arrival at the pound, they lose hope. Again, they are fully aware of what this place is, and they simply lie down in their kennels to die. They don't lift their heads to greet potential adopters. They don't bare their teeth to ward off potential death. Some cower in fear at the back of their kennel, but they make no effort to defend themselves. Others just lie there and put up no resistance at all. I've fostered a few of those, too.

However, I noticed none of this during my first trip through the pound. I was there in response to a call that told me we had thirty minutes before the pound had to start euthanizing to make space. I got permission from the foster committee to go get my first foster dog and drove straight to the pound. From the outside, the small building is quiet and unassuming with only one small window in front and a large fenced area in back. It actually looks like a rather small jail or detention center. Not exactly homey. The parking lot is small, allowing enough space for five or six cars, at best. A few sparse bushes do little to soften the stark white building. I heard nothing aside from a few cars passing on the road behind me as I approached the front door.

I stood at the front door for a moment trying to steal myself for what I was about to do. This was it. This was my moment. I was going to save a life. There would be magical lights and special angel music following me out of the pound as I led the fragile life out of the building of terror and into the joyous land of freedom. I was about to become a freakin super hero. Heroine? That can't be right. Super Woman. Meh. Ok. With a final breath of courage, I put on my imaginary cape, and walked confidently into the pound. It was still eerily quiet in the office area. It almost felt like walking into a dentist's office except for the heavy air of sadness that had settled over the staff. I walked forward and let the woman behind the desk know I was there to save a life.

"You're here to do what?"

"Uhhhh, pull a dog? I'm here to pull a dog. For the humane society. To foster for the humane society. I'm here to pull a dog to foster for the humane society."

"Oh. Ok. Here's the list of pen numbers scheduled to be put down in ten minutes. Do you need me to go with you?"

Not wanting to look like a baby my first time through the pound, I assured the worker that I would be fine. I'd seen the ASPCA commercials, Sarah McLachlan singing sad lyrics while the camera zooms in on terrified, quivering little puppies with enormous sad eyes staring up at you. That stuff tears me apart, and I sob uncontrollably when they come on. I didn't need witnesses to that kind of breakdown. Nope. I was going through there by my damn self.

"Ok, hun. Just let me know which one you want."

Yep. I can do this. I can totally do this. I was going to save a life. This was going to be a great experience. Life changing. Life saving.

I took the list of pen numbers of dogs set to be put down and walked through the door that led from the office area to the hallway. I stood for a moment looking at two more doors, one to my left and one to my right. There was a third open door behind my right shoulder and I could see from where I was standing that it was filled with cat cages. The bulletin board in front of me held photos of lost pets, dozens of them. I looked to my left at the sign on the door labeled "A-Side." Yep. Just like prison. (I should probably point out here that I used to work in prison. My kids tell me that it's important to declare this early on in conversations, as I have the tendency to say things like, "In prison, we used to…" or "You know, the food we had in prison…" Yeah. So, I worked there. I wasn't actually incarcerated. Not that there's anything wrong with that. I mean, there is, obviously, because crime. But also, I mean, rehabilitation and they've served their time and second chances… So, yeah, totally another topic for another book).

So, I looked at the prison-esque A-side door, took another breath, and walked through. Immediately the kennel area came to life. Dogs that were sitting mutely in their kennels suddenly began barking, howling, growling, crying, and jumping up on the kennel doors to see who I was. I looked down at the piece of paper in my hand. Nine dogs were on the list and all would be euthanized in ten minutes. I only had room for one. I stared down a row of fifteen kennels until the din overwhelmed me. This wasn't great. It was the opposite of great. It sucked. It completely sucked. I took hesitant steps down the first row of kennels thinking, "They're all freaking adorable! How am I supposed to pick just ONE???"

Then it dawned on me. I wasn't swooping in to save a life like some super hero. I was deciding which one gets to live and which ones have to die. This wasn't cool. This so wasn't cool. I needed to regroup. I walked back out, stood dumbly by the door, and tried to talk myself through the process.

"Just walk through and don't make eye contact with any of them. Wait. I have to make eye contact. That's how I'll know which one to save. Ok, so make eye contact, but don't pet any of them. Buuuuut, how will I know whether or not they will try to eat my face off when I come near them if I don't try to pet them? Fine. Ok, so make eye contact and pet a few of them. Just don't think about what you're doing. Yeah. Yeah, that sounds like an excellent idea. Don't put any actual thought into which dog you're going to pull from the pound to foster and get adopted. Genius. Pure genius."

I can't really explain how I shut my emotions off or why it worked, but I was eventually able to walk through each row of kennels and interact with each dog on the list without emotionally processing what I was seeing. In my mind I was just walking through a building full of adoptable animals. I stopped and talked to each one, giving head scratches or kissy faces, not entirely certain of what I was looking for. I was so new to animal rescue that I had no idea what made one dog more adoptable than another. I didn't know what criteria other rescuers used to decide which dogs to pull. I was going with my gut. I assumed that when I saw the dog I was supposed to pull, I would know.

I walked through the rows on A-side without any obvious signs of which dog to pull. I walked back through the door into the hallway and continued to hear muffled barking and howling. Three more pen numbers on my list.

I approached the door. B-side was as quiet as A-side had been, but the same chorus of barks and howls roared to life as I pushed the door open. I began my walk down the first row.

And then, suddenly, there he was.

He was probably the least adoptable dog there. He was not a cute little designer breed or a unique larger breed. He was a little odd-looking, and at first glance, there was nothing particularly special about him. He was definitely some sort of Beagle mix, but it was hard to say what he as mixed with. He had long, skinny legs and mismatched whiskers. He was not the dog you use in the sad commercials to encourage donations. He was … goofy. Possibly, he was literally THE Goofy. But he was the one who pleaded with me the most to save him. As soon as I approached his kennel, he stood up on his hind legs, wagged his tail in anticipation, and said, "Oh good, you're here. I was beginning to worry that no one was coming for me."

That was enough for me. Decision made. I went back out to the front desk and announced that I was saving the dog in Pen 21.

"Which one, sweetie? There are two dogs in pen 21. They came in together."

Two. There WERE two dogs in the kennel. I'd seen the second one, but hadn't really processed his presence, or why he would be in a kennel with goofy dog.

"Oh, yeah, um the one with the expressive eyes pleading for a chance to achieve his unfulfilled dreams."

"Ooooookay. So, the brown one or the white one?"

"Um, brown. The brown one."

The pound worker pulled out the paperwork and wrote the name "Buster" at the top of a piece of paper then began filling in boxes. Beagle mix. Two plus years old. Intact. Then she slid the paper around and handed me a pen. I signed the Transfer Authorization, stuck the copy she handed me in my pocket, and prepared my best nurturing voice for this fragile dog they were about to bring out to me. Buster walked out only slightly reluctant to go home with a stranger. He required no coaxing to get him to the car. He may have been confused about who I was, but he seemed very clear on one fact – he was leaving the pound for a better life. I didn't really need my best nurturing voice for him yet. He was going to be just fine.

I'm sure the foster committee was exasperated with me when I told them I'd chosen the odd-looking Beagle mix who was neither house trained nor neutered, had no medical records despite being surrendered by his owner, and who was very intimidated by men. His whiskers were black on one side and white on the other. His legs were a little too long for his body. And he cried like someone was gutting him anytime another dog wandered near. But adoptable or not, he was not going to die that day.

I should point out that Buster had been dumped at the pound, along with another dog, by his person after a reportedly ugly divorce. While the other dog was clearly not a littermate of Buster's, I still refer to him as Buster's brother. They had grown up together and had likely cuddled together while chained outside during severe weather or cowered together at the hands of an angry owner. I cannot say for certain that this is what happened. I can surmise it based on the behaviors that Buster exhibited during the time I fostered him. I didn't save Buster's brother that day, and I did not ask whether or not he made it out of the pound after I left. In my heart I know that he didn't, and I failed in several areas that day. I left Buster's sweet brother behind to die, and because Buster was kenneled together with his brother, I didn't even free up space for the pound to avoid euthanizing. My first attempt at saving lives, and I failed in all respects but one. I saved one life worth saving, one rather unadoptable life.

I brought Buster home and after he finished his five days of mandatory quarantine in my ,basement, I slowly introduced him to my dog Lobo, hoping for the best. I hadn't actually considered this part of fostering, that my dog may not like having random new additions move into the house. I really went into it figuring I would adjust to an extra being in the house and so would everyone else. That was reasonable, right?

Well, probably not. But luckily my first adventures in fostering found the other beings in my house to be exceptionally welcoming to the new additions. I suppose "exceptionally welcoming" may be an exaggeration. Gracie was less than impressed by the idea of having another dog in the house, but she handled it. She didn't complain. In fact, she was completely quiet about it. She simply avoided Buster.

Lobo, however, appeared excited and eager to embrace his new foster brother. His best friend, Rocky, lived across the street and visited regularly to play outside. But since Gracie came to live with us, Rocky was no longer allowed inside the house, and really, blaming Gracie for that rule probably wasn't fair. Rocky and Lobo each weigh a good ninety pounds. That's a lot of dog to have running wide open through my rather small house. It was fine when they were younger and smaller, but my nerves simply couldn't handle it anymore. So, we just told Rocky that he couldn't come in, and we blamed it on the cat. She doesn't care.

For their initial meeting, I brought Lobo down to the basement and let Buster out of his crate. They sniffed each other in greeting and then Lobo looked at me and said, "Sooooo, what? He lives here now? Just like that?"

"Yes, Lobo. Buster is living with us until he finds his forever family."

Lobo looked at Buster. "Dude, you're lost? How can you not have a family? Everyone has a family."

Buster's response, "Uhhh, I gotta pee." And with that, Buster lifted his leg on the closest wall and had at it. Like, he just straight up peed on my basement wall. Not even just on the linoleum floor, but high up on the actual wall. It was actually kind of impressive.

Ok, so this wasn't going to be as easy and glamorous as I imagined. After I finished shrieking and Buster finished running through the rest of the basement in terror while still peeing, I took him outside and explained that we pee outside, not inside. He looked at me with a blank stare and said, "OK. Uhhhh, where's the food?"

Fine. It would just take patience and clear guidance. I could do this.

I spent the next two months picking poop up off my cheap bedroom carpet and scrubbing pee off of my living room walls. I kept Buster crated when I had to go to the store, and I kept him on a regular food and potty schedule. Eventually I was cleaning up poop and pee less and less. Still, Buster didn't like to be crated. After several nights listening to his bone-chilling howls drift up through the basement door, my youngest son moved Buster's crate into his room, thinking it would help him sleep better at night being in the room with him. But Buster cared little about who was in the room with him. When he was in his crate, he would have what can only be described as a doggy conniption. He would flip around inside of the crate until the crate would bounce against the wall. He would then start scooting the bottom of the crate across the carpeted floor until it snagged and ripped the carpet away from the floor. Throughout all of this he would be yowling at top volume, nails scratching against the crate tray.

Within a few days, we had given up the crate altogether and Buster was sleeping in my room. On my bed. Under my covers. He cuddled up as close to me as possible and snored loudly through the night. He was always reluctant to get up in the morning, but quickly fell into routine when he learned that early risers get morning treats.

Then there was the running. Buster was a Beagle. Beagles like to run. On more than one occasion, Buster slipped out of his collar or through the front door, caught a scent, and took off. So off

I'd go after him, commanding him to stop, chasing after him in whatever unfortunate footwear or clothing I managed to grab on my way out the door. Eventually my commanding turned into begging, maybe some crying. Groveling. Obscenities. Usually, during these chases, I was only partially dressed and almost always without shoes. So here I would be, running down the road in my bathrobe, barefoot, and begging at the top of my lungs for this adorable little Beagle to PLEASE STOP RUNNING!

Eventually Buster would find a random tree that he needed to mark, allowing me just enough time to catch up with him. I would pick him up and carry him back home. "Hey, lady. That was a nice morning run, wasn't it? Uhhhhh, why are your feet bleeding like that?"

I couldn't stay mad at him. He was just too cute, in a goofy, not-shaped-quite right kind of way. But it was becoming increasingly clear that he was unlikely to get adopted anytime soon.

He peed all over my house. He cowered in the bathroom when it stormed. He trembled when people approached him. He howled loudly on walks when he caught a scent, and he ran more than once when he managed to slip out the door. He was untrusting of everyone and impossible to keep contained without double-leashing.

But Buster also looked at me gratefully every day knowing that he had been saved. He cuddled close to me on the couch in the evenings. He played gleefully with whatever animal would tolerate him, and he slowly learned that we do not pee on the lady's carpet. He cuddled with me at night and traveled to work with me daily where he patiently allowed the office cat, Cassie, to cuddle with him on the floor. He was quickly playing his way into my heart, and still, I doubted he would ever be adopted. When people call looking for a new pet, they're looking for Chihuahuas and Poodles. When I took Buster to adoption events, he was terrified by the sounds and people surrounding him, so much so that I would have to sit on the ground so he could curl up in my lap to be comforted. There was nothing overtly adoptable about this dog. His specialness was in his soul and you had to look into his eyes to see that.

Then one day I received a call asking if we had any Beagles available for adoption. It was an unexpected call just before Thanksgiving, and though the family was looking for a pure-bred Beagle, I suggested they meet my Beagle mix named Buster. I assured them that if they would only meet him in the calm and quiet of their home, they would fall in love.

So, the next afternoon, Buster and I eagerly visited the home of this wonderful family with three children and a fenced yard where he would be allowed on the furniture and be at no loss for playmates. We knocked on the door, and they welcomed us both inside. I explained apologetically, that Buster was mostly, but not entirely housetrained, so I would keep him on the leash next to me while we talked. The mom insisted that it was not an issue. They had three children and were entirely comfortable with a mess. So, I hesitantly allowed Buster off leash to explore the living room while I explained the adoption process. They had already completed the application and been approved. They simply needed to sign the adoption contract and pay the adoption fee. As I was explaining all of this, Buster was making himself at home. He was calm and quiet as he explored, but also entirely at home. He appeared to feel at ease with this family. And they fell in love with my baby boy. He seemed to enjoy being surrounded by little ones. He found his forever home. Just like that. It was … magical.

We finished the adoption process, and after some time, I decided that Buster was ready for me to leave. I gave him a quick hug and kiss and told him to enjoy his new home. I cried uncontrollably on the way home to mine.

The addiction was set. I needed to save another life.

And I needed to start keeping a box of tissues in my car.

Dammit.

4 A CAT IN A BAG AND A DOG IN A CORNER

It wasn't long after Buster's adoption that I received notice of a kitten found in a trash bag dumped in a shopping center parking lot.

"Seriously? What the hell is wrong with people?"

I really just wanted to knock someone on their ass in response to this news, but me going to jail wouldn't help this little kitten.

A volunteer directed the family that found the kitten to bring him to our office where I would process him into our foster program. That evening, a woman and her young son brought a purring and inquisitive little orange tabby cat into my office and sat him down on my desk. He immediately began exploring. Because of the location he was found, the family had been calling him Wally and oddly enough, this name seemed to fit him. When I picture a "Wally," I picture a somewhat aloof teenage boy just kind of hanging out at the back of the room not because he's awkward and shy, but because he doesn't need to be the center of attention. Wally wasn't exactly aloof. He was very responsive to petting and cuddling, but he had this air of coolness about him that told you he was not one of the fragile broken ones.

"Huh? Oh, yeah, I was at some house, and this dude picked me up, put me in a bag, and took me to the Walmarts. I thought we were going shopping for mousey toys and stuff, but then he just tied the bag up and dropped me in the parking lot. It was hard to breathe in that bag, and I couldn't get out no matter how hard I tried. I probably could have died, but I didn't, so it's all good."

There is clearly a life lesson to be learned from this little boy's response to life's hardships. If that mess didn't kill you, then just deal with it and move on. Don't linger.

It was precisely Wally's view of the world that told me he would be fine to move on to a new home whenever the time came. Still, I tried not to become attached to him. We all tried. But Wally was one of those special cats that everyone loves, even those that claim not to like cats.

I took him home to foster because, much like Gracie, I didn't like the idea of him alone at the office over the weekends. And we continued to struggle to find foster homes for cats. Because he had spent his mandatory quarantine period at our office, I didn't bother to keep him separated from Gracie for any period of time. I was still unversed in cat behavior and knew nothing about introducing cats slowly. Where I grew up, cats lived outside among whatever other animals happened to live in that area. You didn't really know what they did or how they responded to other animals when you weren't around, and really, you weren't around a lot. I don't remember really thinking of cats as pets. Dogs were pets. Cats were … there.

So, when I brought Wally home, I just threw him in the mix with Lobo and Gracie, and he immediately made himself at home, quickly claiming the laundry basket as his bed. He didn't care whether it contained clean clothes or dirty. He was content either way, and either his youth or his non-confrontational personality led Gracie and Lobo to accept his claim on our home.

Not long after I brought Wally home, another little one walked into my office and, thus, into my life. Slim Shady was a tiny, fragile-looking Italian Greyhound that stood trembling behind the legs of the woman that found him wandering the cold city streets in the dead of winter. She brought him to the humane society because she couldn't find his owner, and she didn't want to take him to the pound. For that, I am thankful. This little man would have been beyond terrified in the pound. He was beyond terrified standing in the calm setting of the humane society office.

The woman sat Slim on the floor, and he immediately found the farthest corner in the room away from me and made himself as small as he could. And he shook. And he trembled. And he clearly did everything in his power to disappear. I convinced the woman that Slim would be fine. I would take great care of him and find him the perfect forever home. Yeah, because it would be that easy.

After she left, I sat there at my desk looking at Slim. He sat cowering in the corner looking anywhere but at me.

"Hey little guy. You wanna come over here and see me?"

Silence.

"A treat? You want a treat?"

Silence.

Clearly I was intimidating him by sitting in the chair. I should get on the floor and get closer to him. Apparently I thought cornering a terrified dog behind a desk with no means of escape would be comforting to him. I got down on my hands and knees and peered over at him.

"Hey little man, come out and see me!"

Now, to his credit, Slim never growled at me. Still, as I lay there half under the desk reaching out to this tiny, shaking skeleton of a dog, an air of dread settled over the room. Maybe this wasn't the best approach. I know what you're thinking, "How has this woman managed to survive working around animals without losing a limb?" Well, to be honest, I'm not quite sure.

I slowly backed out from under the desk and climbed back up into my chair. I went back to work and ignored Slim. I sat in silence for nearly an hour. I actually forgot that the little guy was even there until he ventured out from his corner behind the desk and began to slowly explore the room. He made great, sweeping circles of the area gradually working his way toward me. If I made the mistake of looking in his direction or holding out my hand for him to smell, he retreated back under the desk. More ignoring and he eventually built up the courage to approach me.

"So, um, you, uhhh, you're my person now?" Slim said in a small, shaky voice.

"I'm your foster momma. You're gonna stay with me until we can find you a forever home."

"Oh. So you don't want me either."

"Oh, no no no sweet little boy!"

I gently picked Slim up and cuddled him and assured him that we would find him a forever home that would be so much better than mine. He would get love and cuddles and playtime all the time, and he would be safe forever.

After that, Slim rarely left my arms. If I was sitting, he was cuddled in my lap. If I was sleeping, he was cuddled under the covers next to me. If I was walking to the car, he was cuddled in my arms. If I was driving—

"Dude. No. You have GOT to sit in your own seat while I drive."

"Ok. Ok. But just please don't park the car on some deserted road and act like you're just going to step out to get something and then just run away abandoning me in the car, k?"

Ok. So he was still very skittish, making it increasingly difficult to find him a forever home. One thing did give him an advantage over some of our other foster dogs. Slim loved cats, especially Wally. Probably because they were the same size. They would romp and play constantly. When they were tired from playing, they would both curl up on the back of the chair in the sun. It was the few times Slim would give me any space, and when Wally was adopted and Gracie refused to stoop so low as to play with a dog, Slim turned to Lobo for a playmate. So there was Slim, ten pounds of skin and bones wrestling with Lobo, ninety pounds of muscle. So, this tiny little dog that was initially so terrified of me in all of my gentleness never hesitated to take on a monster of a dog in a wrestling match. It was adorable, and it was terrifying. And they wouldn't stop no matter how much I begged. To his credit, though, Lobo was able to balance rough play with a gentle touch and was never in danger of hurting this tiny thing. Dogs are so much smarter than us.

I had concerns that Slim might never get adopted. He was really the perfect small dog. He didn't yip. In fact, he rarely made a sound. He loved cats. And he was a cuddler. But when I would take him places, he would immediately start trembling and attempt to disappear into my arms as strangers approached. I began to feel like Paris Hilton carrying this designer dog around with me everywhere. Also, Slim tested positive for heartworms which meant he would require extensive treatments to be fully healthy. One family that had expressed interest in him backed out when they found out about his diagnosis. Another family came to meet him, and Slim refused to come near them. They spent an hour on the floor trying to coax him with treats, and he simply shook and hid behind my legs. I was just unwilling to adopt him out to a family he was unable to adjust to very quickly. I know. It seems unfair, and he probably would have been fine. Eventually. But sometimes you just know when they know. Just when I'd given up hope for him to find his forever family, Slim's forever mom walked through the door.

Don't misunderstand. She had never met Slim before, but as soon as she walked in and sat down on the floor, Slim climbed into her lap and kissed her face. He picked his forever momma, as rescued animals often will. She visited him a few more times before her application was completed and approved. It was beautiful watching them together, the way he knew instinctively that this was the person he could trust to be there for him the rest of his life the way he would be there for her. It was exhilarating.

On the day of his adoption, as his new momma was walking him to her car, Slim glanced back at me and said, "Thanks so much for all you've done, but I'm going home now."

I cried when they pulled out of the driveway.

As I mentioned, Wally was also adopted shortly before Slim was. He received only one adoption application, but it was a good one. My kids and I had all grown quite attached to the little guy. I mean, he didn't really take over our home or push his way into our hearts. He just simply existed in time with our family and seemed a natural part of our home. My kids weren't entirely happy to hear that we'd found an adopter for him. Without much fanfare, he went to live with a sweet older couple who wanted a playmate for their other cat. As I had known from the start, Wally was perfectly fine leaving me and walked out of my life with grace and confidence. He was going to be fine, regardless how much it hurt me to part with him. I knew it was the best for him and for the opportunity it would give other animals that needed a place to crash while waiting for their forever homes.

So, with Wally and Slim adopted, I had some space. We had recently taken in a pretty little calico cat at headquarters when her owner was no longer able to care for her. Pumpkin's owner had lost her home and had to move from place to place, struggling to make ends meet. Every new place she stayed, she had to keep Pumpkin crated with less and less free time. When she finally ended up living in her car, Pumpkin's owner made the heart-wrenching decision to surrender Pumpkin to us in hopes she would be adopted into a stable, loving home. Again, we had no open foster homes, so Pumpkin initially had to stay in an upstairs room at headquarters. Since I only worked 16 hours a week, Pumpkin received very little human interaction.

Our medical advisor, Lexi, warned me that Pumpkin was a very aggressive cat and that I should take care when feeding her, being careful not to handle her. Yet, when I would enter the room, she was cautious, but gentle. Pumpkin didn't purr, but she did allow me to pet her. Eventually, she even sought me out for pets. She craved love and attention. Ok. Maybe "crave" is too strong a word. Pumpkin didn't crave anything, except possibly human blood, but she did accept attention. To me that was the same as adoring me.

Pumpkin was clearly unaccustomed to spending so much time alone, so when the space opened up at my house, I suggested that she come stay with me. She started out in the basement away from Gracie and Lobo, and the rest of us, quite honestly. She was anxious all the time and did not want to be near any of us. The semi-sweet girl I met at headquarters was nowhere to be found in my basement. She had been replaced by a vicious, angry beast that struck fear into the hearts of every member of my family. Most of us avoided the basement as much as possible. Of course, she needed food and water and a clean litter box, so at least once a day, I had to creep cautiously down the stairs, careful not to upset her majesty, and care for her food and bathroom needs. I always announced myself before entering, kept my head down, careful not to make eye contact and shuffled quickly in and out of rooms. I was skulking around in my own home like a criminal stealing poo out of litter boxes and bowing down like a servant.

It took weeks before she would venture upstairs without hissing and growling at all of us. In truth, it took weeks before I was willing to keep the basement door open and risk her venturing upstairs with the rest of us. For our own safety I thought it best to keep that barrier secure. I mean, we gotta sleep, right? And I damn sure wasn't closing my eyes around her.

But I finally relented, figuring the longer she was isolated from society, the worse her social skills would become. We had isolation in prison. You didn't want to be in isolation. Pumpkin gradually crept upstairs and began to explore the new surroundings. She made sure to hiss and growl at every living being she encountered, lest we mistake her for a cuddler and attempt physical contact. Little did she know that none of us had any desire to cuddle with her. We avoided her at all costs.

Eventually, though, something began to change in Pumpkin. She was hissing less and spending more and more time adjacent to one of us. Then one day as I was on the couch watching TV, I felt an odd presence next to me. I turned carefully expecting to see a snarling calico cat, instead finding a tranquil Pumpkin curled up beside me enjoying the day. I wasn't quite sure how to react. I wanted to be indignant. How are you going to spend months acting superior to me and hissing at me and treating me like a servant in my own home and then one day just decide we can cuddle like nothing ever happened? How are you going to just play with my emotions like that? Who do you think you are?

I couldn't be indignant. I was excited and grateful. I had earned her trust. She liked me! She really liked me! This is how cats turn us into 13-year old children begging for attention from the popular kids. And it wasn't just me.

She also quickly established her dominance in the house, letting Gracie and Lobo know that she was not to be trifled with. In fact, we quickly discovered that Pumpkin had some feline form of bipolar disorder. Much like the at-risk youth I worked with in previous jobs, Pumpkin would be sweet and calm one moment and turn and growl at you the next. It was never clear what would set her off. She would go from purring to hissing in a second. It was these fluctuations in character that led to her various nicknames: Punky, Punky Brewster, Punky Pants, Punk Rock, CM Punk, Punk Punk, and even Pissy Pants Punky when she was being especially mean.

It became abundantly clear that this pretty little cat was not going to be easy to get adopted. She settled into a routine, and our home became her home. I mean it literally became her home. She actually declared that this was her home, and she allowed us to stay here, probably only because I was the one who knew how to open the cans of food. She acted as though she had no intentions of ever leaving.

A few months after Punky took over the deed to the house (while I continued to pay the actual mortgage), I received a call about a litter of 3-week old kittens left motherless when their momma was hit by a car. Knowing that we are usually able to send kittens out of state for adoption and that they would probably die without appropriate care, this was an easy decision. I would foster them. How hard could it be to bottle-feed three adorable little babies? When I thought of kittens, I had images of sweet little balls of fluffy fur with bright eyes and cute whiskers. When I arrived to pick them up, that is definitely not what I found.

"So, what are you handing me here? Is this a box full of, what, poop balls? Are they, maybe some form of parasite? Are there warnings, like, maybe I shouldn't expose them to the light or feed them after midnight? My GAWD what is that smell?"

When the lady explained that these were the kittens she had called about ,and no she didn't have poop on her, I looked suspiciously back into the box. Yep. That sure is where the smell is coming from. Good Lord, they were … gross. There was nothing cuddly about them. Why would anyone ever want one of these?

Then I caught sight of two little blue crust-covered eyes and I picked up the smelly box and carried it to my car. Our first stop would have to be the vet's office to make sure they would survive the night. I needed feeding supplies. The clawing sounds coming from the backseat of my car during the drive was a little unnerving. I just knew they were going to escape and start climbing over me with their Freddy Krueger claws and muck-covered paws. But we made to it the vet's office without incident, and I carried the smelly box inside for our vet to check them over.

I held my breath while she looked doubtfully into the box and then up at me and then back into the box. She pursed her lips as she picked one of the muck-balls up out of the box and appeared to be trying to decide something. Although she clearly doubted their health, she saw the hope in my eyes and shook her head.

"Ok. Here's what you need to do." She proceeded to give me detailed instructions on how to bottle feed them, clean them, and keep them quarantined from my other cats until we were sure they were healthy.

"Wait. So, I have to wipe their private parts every time I feed them? Isn't that, you know, questionable behavior? Shouldn't that be a no-go area?"

Apparently you have to wipe a newborn kitten's pee pee area to stimulate them otherwise they won't go to the bathroom. They'll just hold it. Like, forever, I guess. Or until they explode in a rain of matted fur and cat piss. I promise I'm not making this up. I mean, I haven't actually researched the pee rain thing, but I figure there's a pretty good chance that I'm right. Google it.

I took them home and set up a crate in my bathroom. They waited impatiently in the box as I set up a little litter box, water dish, and clean, cuddly blankets for them. I made sure everything was perfect before I began to feed and clean them and move them into the pristine cage. One by one, I took them out of the box and fed them warm kitten milk replacer with a syringe. I washed each one with a warm washcloth, making sure to clean every part of them. One by one, they transformed into the sweet little balls of fluffy fur with bright eyes and cute whiskers that I had pictured before seeing them for the first time. I placed them into their clean, cozy, comfortable crate and encouraged them to take a nap. I closed the door as I left them in the bathroom and went outside to clean the muck that had leaked out of the box into my car during the ride. When I came back inside to check on the fluffers several minutes later, I was shocked at the scene in my bathroom. How had they thrown wet litter all the way across the room? The crate door was closed. How did they transform back into the grimy, messy near-skeletons? Where were the sweet little balls of fluffy fur with bright eyes and cute whiskers? When did the mini-monsters come back? Gross. Kittens are gross. They are messy. They are loud, and they stink. They are worse than teenage boys. For the next two months, my bathroom would smell and sound, like the bathroom at a college frat party, only way less fun.

And I would treasure every moment.

We named the kittens Piper, Peppers, and Pierre, but to me, they were the Stinky Butts. Feeding times came every 2-3 hours, and I was quickly reminded of why I stopped at two children. I need my sleep, and midnight feedings are highly inconvenient. We made it through the weeks and the Stinky Butts grew bigger, stronger, and more ornery.

Every time I entered my bathroom, they swarmed me. I had quickly lost the heart to keep them crated throughout the day, so they had full roam of the bathroom. It really didn't make much difference as far as cleanliness. Kittens can make a mess out of anything within a four-foot radius of whatever crate they are being contained in. As I dried my hair, kittens scaled my legs. Even as the weather grew hotter, I was forced to wear jeans. My legs already looked like I'd had more than one run-in with Freddy Krueger. I was a human scratching post.

And Pissy Pants Punky was entirely disgusted that I would bring such drivel into her home. She would sit at the top of the stairs and growl in the direction of the bathroom. She didn't know what I had in there, but she knew they were not appropriate companions for the likes of her.

"Why are they here? Where is their mother and when is she coming to get them?"

Gracie, on the other hand, sat protectively outside the door looking concerned and worried.

"There are babies in there and I know they need me. They shouldn't be left alone. Where is their momma?"

The Stinky Butts eventually grew into healthy, fluffy, bright-eyed kittens, each with a unique personality.

Peppers was the explorer. He was the first to figure out how to reach the toilet paper so they could trail it around the bathroom. He was the one who found a way, and I still don't know how, to get onto the sink, the new location for the toilet paper, so they could trail it around the bathroom. He is the one who would scale the length of my body until he was standing on top of my head while I brushed my teeth in the morning.

Piper was the playful one. She loved toys, any toys. She would play chase the flying fish nonstop until I thought my arms would fall off from holding the stick in the air. She forced her brothers to play, rolling them around when they were trying to relax.

Pierre was my baby. He would start purring like a motor boat the moment I walked into the room. He just wanted to be with me all the time. He also had an unfortunate skin condition that disqualified him from going on the kitten transport for adoption, which was the original plan for this litter. He would require some treatment for that condition before he could go on the transport.

Several weeks later, when our kitten coordinator called and asked me to bring Peppers and Piper for transport in the morning, I was struck with mixed emotions. I would miss the little Stinky Butts that were leaving me, and I hated to separate them from their brother. While I was happy to still have my little Pierre with me, I dreaded the day when he would have to go on the transport by himself without the comfort of his brother and sister.

The day they were to leave me forever, I packed Piper and Peppers into a carrier, Pierre looking on in confusion.

"But where my brother and sister go without me? Where they go with you and not me?"

Damn this was gonna be hard. I closed the bathroom door behind me, not wanting to leave Pierre alone at the hands of Punky, and carried his siblings out to my car. We drove to the library in eerie silence as though they knew I was not happy about what I was doing. I don't remember if I said goodbye to them. Honestly, I only remember hurriedly getting them from my car and handing the carrier over to the coordinator and thinking, "My dear God, how does she do this over and over again?"

I also remember holding back the tears until I was safely back in my car and out of sight. The obvious confusion in their eyes as I was putting them in the carrier without their brother was more than I could take. One fear of every foster parent is that the little one you are sending off to their wonderful new forever family will, even for a second, think they've done something wrong and that you don't love them anymore. Although I like to think that they will remember me forever, I am comforted by the knowledge that those responsible for choosing their forever home have found them a family that gives them so much love that they will never have a need to think of me.

Yes, I cried like a baby the whole way home, and then I cuddled with my Pierre.

6 I Thought We Kept Those In The Bathroom

Over the next several weeks, my home fell into a rhythm. Pierre took to calling me momma. He had settled into his role in the family and was now allowed access to the full house. Initially, Punky was appalled by this.

"I thought we kept those things locked in the bathroom so people wouldn't know we had them."

However she eventually resigned herself to accepting his presence and he became part of the natural cadence of our home.

It was fall now, and on a beautiful, cool morning following weeks of stifling heat and humidity, I love opening doors and windows to allow a fresh breeze through while I enjoy my morning coffee. I always envision those coffee commercials with picturesque views and serene mornings. That's what my life used to be. My life before animal rescue, but also not when my kids were too young. It was in that sweet spot between pre-adolescent children and animal fostering. Now, here is what I get instead:

Lobo:
"A car! Mom, I hear a car! A car is coming, I hear it! A car is turning down our road! It's a car! I don't know whose car, but it's a car! A car! A car!"

Me:
"Lobo, please stop barking. It's just a car."

Punky:
"Look at how elegantly I can climb up this screen door. All the way to the top. I look just like a pretty ballerina when I climb like this."

Me:
"Punky, please get off the screen before you tear it."

Lobo:

"A deer! Mom, I hear a deer! A deer is coming! I can hear it! A deer is coming into our yard! It's a deer! I don't know this deer, but it's a deer! A deer! A deer!"

Me:

"Lobo, please stop barking. It's just a deer."

Gracie:

"Look at me…ugh…climb…*gasp*…up…the…scr-"

Punky:

"Move out of my way, fatty butt. This is how you climb."

Me:

"Gracie and Punky, please STOP climbing on the screen!"

Lobo:

"An airplane! Mom, I hear an airplane! There's an airplane! Airplane! Airplane!"

Me:

"Lobo! For the love of all that is good, PLEASE STOP barking! It's JUST a freakin airplane!"

Pierre:

"Momma? What is this stuff in your mug? Can I have some? It looks…ow!"

Me:

"Pierre, please leave my coffee alone."

Me:

"Gracie, please get your butt off the screen before you bust it, AGAIN."

Gracie:

"What? I'm just laying here enjoying the breeze."

Punky:

"Move out of the way, fatty butt. I want to sit in the window."

Lobo:

"Rocky! Mom, I see Rocky! Rocky's outside! It's Rocky! Can I go outside and play with Rocky?"

Me:

"Ugh! Fine! JUST go outside and play with Rocky and stop barking please!"

Pierre:

"Momma! Be careful! Don't drink that! It's HOT!"

Lobo:

"Mom! It's me and Rocky! I'm playing with Rocky, mom! Mom! Can Rocky and I come inside and play?"

Rocky:

"Ms. Sunshine! Are those cats? Can I come inside and play with the cats?"

Punky:

"Ew. Another dog. They're so gross. Please don't let them in here, lady."

Pierre:

"I'm serious momma! That stuff is hot! It will burn your nose!"

Gracie:

"No, mom! I wasn't tearing the screen away from the door. That was the dogs doing that!"

Yep. Serene, peaceful morning. *sigh*

7 The Day My Windows Shut Forever

In response to my whining about not being able to sit and enjoy my morning coffee with the windows open, my mother gave me some double-sided sticky tape to put on my windowsills. She assured me that her cats likened it to some sort of evil that had risen up out of the depths of hell, so it would no doubt be effective in keeping my cats away from the screens. She didn't have any suggestions for keeping Lobo from announcing every being approaching within a five-mile radius. But at least the cats would stop busting out the window screens. Except that her cats are not my cats. Her cats are, for the most part, normal. (Read, boring.)

I had never tried this stuff in the past because it always sounded a little torturous to me. Kind of like fly paper. Effective, but cruel. However, a lack of adequate coffee intake was enough to push me to try it. I mean, what is crueler than denying a thirty-something working single mother of her morning coffee? (As I edit this book for final publication, I am now a forty-something single mother of two grown-ass men. Damnit.)

I carried my sticky tape happily back home certain I had found my solution. My cats, sensing my victorious air, followed me around suspiciously as I applied the sticky tape to the first windowsill.

Punky, in her best Stewie voice:
"Whatcha doin there, lady? You applying some sticky tape there, are ya? You got some sticky tape there? Yeah? You putting a little bit of sticky tape down there? Huh? Some sticky tape? Just a little sticky tape on the windows there? Just putting some sticky tape on the windows? Hmm? Just a little sticky tape? Yeah? Yeah? No, really, you deserve some peace in the mornings."

Despite Punky's obvious sarcasm, I continued to apply sticky tape to the other windowsills.

Pierre:

"What's that, momma? Why are you doin that, momma? Is that a cleaner, momma? Is it for decoration, momma? Can I see, momma? What...sticky! Fun! This is fun, momma! Look! It's sticky! Look, momma! When I stand up here, I can't fall! Thank you, momma! This is so fun! Thank you for the sticky!"

Ok, he's young and hasn't learned that sticky paws are unpleasant. He's not the one busting out screens, anyway. I proceeded to apply sticky tape to the screen door, my main area of concern as Gracie has already managed to pull the lower section away from the actual frame.

Gracie:

"Um, yeah, sooooo sticky tape. Yeah. So, you don't want me to open the door that way anymore, huh? But I suppose it's ok that the neighbor dog climbs up there every time he's over, huh? Yeah. No no. I totally understand."

Ok, well the sticky tape did nothing to deter the cats from pushing through the screens, but it did serve to patch the holes they had made over the past year. And really, I can just drink my coffee outside.

Still, there are times when you simply have to open the windows and let the air circulate. This is especially imperative in homes where animals and teenage boys reside. I recently had to issue a Code Fur, again. For those without strictly indoor cats, let me clarify what a Code Fur is. You'll need this knowledge if you ever spend any amount of time in my home, specifically during the open window months.

A Code Fur occurs when one of the cats, usually the chubby one named Gracie, manages to bust one of the screens out of the window, resulting in a mass cat exodus from inside my home.

Generally, the bipeds in the house are alerted to the situation by a loud clattering sound and Lobo tattling with loud panicky barks.

(I should note that, since the original writing of this chapter, I no longer issue Code Furs. Three of the screens in my home have large flappy corners torn away from the frame, so pretty much any animal smaller than a large fox can come and go from my home as they please in the spring and fall. I no longer restrict the cats. If those little assholes want to go outside, they can go. They're too damn lazy to run far, anyway. They lay around on the porch until it's time to come back inside for more food. Gracie will occasionally leave the porch to hunt, capture, and bring a baby mole back for dinner. But that's, like, once a year and at least she's trying to contribute. The rest of them pretty much just lay around getting fatter all damn day.)

In the past, our Code Fur responses were very reminiscent of the Three Stooges episode where Larry has to get the cats out of the piano. They are most likely to occur when we are least able to manage them appropriately. In fact, I am usually home alone, running frantically around the house yelling, "Code Fur! Code Fur!" to no one in particular and diving into the pantry to get a can of cat food. The real trick to successful handling of a Code Fur is to time the opening of the can of cat food so that the cats hear it and come running. Normally, they have headed straight for the woods that surround the house, so you don't have a clear indication of which side of the house to be on when you open the can of cat food.

(Again, if you don't chase them and freak the hell out, it's no longer fun for them. Ignore bad behavior, people!)

(Plus, I think they were catching on to my use of food to lure them back and were actually just using these "escapes" as a way to get second breakfast.)

If you're lucky enough to get that piece right, then you have the added challenge of attempting to gather two or three cats up in your arms and carry them back into the house without losing an eye...or an arm. There is a reason that the term "herding cats" is an actual term.

This particular morning, the Code Fur came just before the boys were supposed to leave for school. Fortunately, since this was actually our 1000th Code Fur of the year, we responded efficiently and effectively, allowing for only one escapee. One boy took up position by the compromised point of exit, preventing cats numbers two and three from escaping. The other boy took up a flanking position around the side of the house. I grabbed a can of cat food and practiced my sweet voice as I approached the subject. (Yeah, I have to practice my sweet voice. It doesn't come naturally.)

I popped open the can of food and Punky immediately came running to me. As Damon scooped her up and carried her back inside, I could hear her cursing,

"You have won this time, human. This time."

I think it's best that we just keep the windows closed from here on out.

8 Poo-Covered Beagles and Jungle Tarantulas

About the time the kittens left me, Mindy and I began visiting the pound weekly to take photos and get more information on the animals there. We would move slowly from pen to pen, taking photos, interacting with the dogs and cats, and collecting whatever limited details pound staff had on each animal. Those details were extremely limited. That's understandable when a dog comes in as a stray, but so many of these animals are surrendered by their owners without even basic information like age and spay/neuter status. Asking for vet records is pointless. I mean, I'm mostly going to judge you if you're surrendering your pet to the pound in anything but the most extreme circumstances. If you're doing so without even giving them a fighting chance, then you're mostly just a waste of resources. We posted the photos and whatever information we could obtain on our Humane Society Facebook page in hopes that even one of them would be adopted, fostered, or reclaimed by their owner. Each visit found us facing several scared little faces, most of which had been surrendered by their "families."

And again, I get it. Families surrender pets for different reasons. Sometimes they're facing hardships like job loss, eviction, hospitalization, military deployment. Situations that are devastating enough in and of themselves, only to be compounded by having to send your baby to their likely death, scared and alone, inside a pound. My heart hurts for those people and I've heard the tears of relief in their voice when I've called them to tell them that we'd pulled their baby out of the pound, and he or she was safe in a loving foster home waiting for adoption. They had cared enough to leave their contact information in hopes that someone would rescue their baby and they wanted to be able to answer whatever questions that person had. Sadly, those stories are not the majority.

Most times, I have found that their reasoning is less understandable. They no longer have time for the animal. The puppy is destroying their house. The dog got too big. The cat keeps peeing on their bed. They're pregnant now and don't know how to handle both a pet and a newborn. The dog got pregnant, and they don't have room for puppies. The dog snapped at their toddler after the kid pulled its tail or tried to ride it like it was a freakin horse.

Seriously. Here is my response to these "reasons." Make the time. Train the puppy (because why in the hell did you get a puppy if you weren't prepared to train it? Puppies chew things. Everything. They're puppies. Who in the hell doesn't already know this???) A Labrador puppy starts out small, but will potentially grow to be 90 lbs. because dogs, like humans and every other animal, grow as they age from newborn to adulthood. (Again, seriously? Do you not understand this?) FIX YOUR PETS!!!! Seriously. There are low-cost spay/neuter programs all over the damn country. USE THEM! Talk to a damn veterinarian. Cats pee in the wrong places for behavioral or medical reasons. I get it. Cat pee is THE single worst smell you will ever smell in your life, but it's fixable. Do some research. Dogs, cats, and a host of other animals can live peacefully with a baby. If you're not motivated enough to monitor your pets around your child, then I'm gonna go ahead and suggest that you probably shouldn't be producing children. Because do NOT, ever, no matter how patient your pet, allow your freakin child to climb all over them like they're a damn jungle gym. Don't let them pull their tail or stick their hands in their mouths. Basically, teach your child to be a decent human being with respect for other life forms. Teach them not to be an asshole. If you can manage that little parenting task, I probably won't have to talk to you about your child's probation requirements in the future.

Anyway, when Mindy and I arrived at the pound on this particular day, we were notified that the pound would have to euthanize eight dogs that day because they were out of space. So off we went with our cameras and pads of paper to see who we could find. What we found was way more adoptable dogs than we had room for.

We found Trixie, a young Boxer mix that was thankfully taken in by our selfless and inspiring friends at a small upstart rescue. We found Annie Mae, an attention-starved Lab mix who was saved by one of our amazing fosters who manages to place even the most unlikely of dogs into the perfect homes. We found Lola, another young Boxer mix and Rocky & Skippy, two energetic young Lab mixes. All three were saved by another of our tireless fosters to wait for transport to another rescue organization with seemingly endless access to wonderful, loving adopters.

And we found Lucky, a roly-poly Beagle/Chihuahua mix who came waddling and wagging up to the front of the kennel to greet us. The first thing that struck me about this boy was his pure, unalterable joy with life. Here was this pudgy little guy suddenly without his person, stuck in a cold, lonely kennel surrounded by barking and sadness and chaos. He was on the list of dogs set to die in less than an hour, and don't think for a second that they don't know when they are on that list. They know. Lucky's response?

"Hi there, ladies! How are you today? It's such a beautiful day, isn't it? I mean, I haven't been outside yet today, but I just know it's a beautiful day! Are you enjoying this beautiful day? I hope you're having a wonderful, beautiful day!"

How do you walk away from that? Any being that can react so positively to such a devastating fate can bring nothing but happiness to anyone lucky enough to have him in their life. There was no question that Lucky was coming home with me. I needed some positivity in my life, and he was just too cute and wiggly to walk away from.

So I packed up this little piggly wiggly and took him home. He was a little on the chubby side thanks to a lifetime diet of table scraps. By agreeing to come home with me, Lucky unwittingly entered my boot camp. He had some pounds to shed to get back to a healthy weight, and it was going to be work. His next few weeks were filled with diet food and two-a-day walks, but he never complained once. He was just gleefully happy to be out of jail and safe.

Lucky was also one of the few that was so loved by his surrendering person that she left her contact information with the pound. When I called this sweet elderly woman to tell her that Lucky was now with me in my home where I would love and cuddle and foster him until we could find a wonderful adoptive home for him, she broke down sobbing. I allowed her to cry, and after several minutes, she managed to simply say thank you. That is all the fuel you need to continue doing this work, because I can only hope that if I am ever in such a devastating position that I have no other options left to me but to send my pets to the pound, someone will rescue them from that hell. That would likely be the only way I could manage through whatever crisis I was facing.

A few days in, the Richards Family Foster Boot Camp was in full swing, and Lucky seemed to be adjusting. I, however, was struggling a bit. Each day, Lucky and I had walked a short little loop around my neighborhood, no more than ½ a mile. I decided that Lucky was ready to walk a bit further on his fourth morning with me, so we ventured out of my immediate neighborhood and up on to the rather hilly main road. Lucky was very excited about the new smells that the main road brings. Foxes and squirrels and deer and damn raccoons wander around up there, and I've even heard Lobo mention bear smells every now and then. Keep in mind that this wildlife spends a great deal of time in my yard, as is evidenced by the state of my trash cans and tomato plants every morning, but apparently the smells are either much stronger or much more interesting up on the main road.

On our walks, I tried to at least keep him on the grassy shoulder beside the road so we wouldn't be surprised by snakes or Tarantulas or chupacabras. One would not think that an out-of-shape Chihuahua mix could exert much strength during a long walk, but Lucky was dissatisfied with the grassy area and was intent on walking along the tree line to really get the full effect of country living. He wasn't taking no for an answer.

About ten minutes into our walk, he found some fresh poo to roll in. I was appalled as I watched him really grind his face and neck

47

into it. Of course, I couldn't physically stop him, because that would require touching him and therefore also touching the foreign poo. (I'm not sure why the fact that it was foreign needed to be pointed out here except that I spend so much time with the known poo of my own pets on or around me that I almost don't even notice it anymore so I guess the fact that the poo was foreign to me is what stopped me from stopping him. So, yeah. Yeah, it totally makes sense to point it out here.)

Since I couldn't stop him from really digging into the foreign poo, my only other logical option was to shriek in horror and run ahead. Oddly enough, it worked because he popped up quite spryly for such a pudgy thing and looked concerned.

"What's wrong with you, lady? Did ya get bit or somethin?"

I stammered out something about gross and bath and why in the hell would you roll in that mess. About the time Lucky decided that I was just a freak and he'd best just follow me and leave the poo for another day, I walked smack into the largest spider web I've ever encountered. The web stretched the entire length of my body and led to more intense shrieking, lots of cursing, a wild little Kung Fu type dance, and perhaps some clothing removal. At that point, Lucky decided to find some more poo and pretend not to know me. The shrieking wasn't about to end until I was certain that the jungle-sized Tarantula that was no doubt lurking in my hair was no longer on my person. My dad has told me stories about the wildlife in the jungles of Vietnam, and I'm certain that this spider was an import and must have been at least the size of my head. However, ensuring said spider was safely off of me meant stripping down a bit and shaking my hair wildly and, of course, some shrieking. I'm not sure how not a single other living being happened by at this point, but short of sharing this story with you, I might have just walked away gracefully and pretended it never happened. Those who know me will attest, I am incapable of not sharing. It's a compulsion, and one I've never really bothered to fight.

After about ten minutes of searching and swiping and spinning and shrieking, I felt satisfied that I was not carrying any foreign bodies and decided it best that we just head back home. I was exhausted, apparently, so was Lucky. Because he took about five steps then stopped dead in his tracks and laid down in the grass looking at the hill in front of us and then back at me like I was more than welcome to go on without him.

I had two options, drag him along by his leash all the way up the hill or carry his poo-covered body. At this point, I was exhausted, traumatized, and anxious to get home to my shower. Since I had to shower anyway…

We avoided the tree line on all future walks.

9 THE POWER SHIFT

The moment I began fostering, the hierarchy of power in my home began shifting based on the foster animals that were coming and going. I should point out that through all of these power shifts neither of *my* babies ever held the power. Both Gracie and Lobo tend to prefer a life free of drama and so are content to allow whatever random foster shows up in their home to dictate their place in the house. (I tend to have a similar response to dating, which is why I've decided I really just shouldn't do it.) Yes, even the ninety pound Lobo would prefer to scrounge around in the trash that the damn raccoons string across the yard every night rather than challenge a ten-week old kitten standing in the general proximity of his food bowl.

For six months, Punky had been the queen bee in charge of EVERYONE. She determined seating arrangements and dictated feeding schedules, all to suit her liking. Despite the fact that she was, in fact, the smallest being in this house, she had the largest personality and all of the control...until 6:08am, August 31st, 2011.

At 6:07am, I was sleeping peacefully, if not comfortably, in my bed surrounded by Lobo, Lucky, and Punky. At 6:08am, I was shielding my face from an appalled Punky who was being put firmly in her place by Stinky Butt Pierre. I had taken to calling him Stinky Butt as a kitten, as I do all kittens. His nickname continued to be an accurate label even as he grew, though I had hoped that a trip to remove his boy-parts would change that. It didn't.

At any rate, our morning routine was fairly consistent.

Normally, Punky would swat or growl or generally intimidate away from me any other being that dared approach my head in the morning. It wasn't that she felt any sort of affection or closeness to me. It was that I apparently need my head to wake me up and get her breakfast ready. So, every morning when Stinky Butt would come bounding in yelling, "Momma! Wake up, momma! It's a BEAUTIFUL DAY, momma! Wake up and enjoy it," Punky would smack him firmly across the face in an attempt to beat the positivity out of him and get him away from the head that needed to focus on making her breakfast. Stinky would then slouch back, always appearing shocked and hurt, and slink away to sit by my feet waiting patiently, and quietly, for my head to go make Punky's breakfast.

On the morning of August 31st, 2011, Stinky came bounding in yelling, "Momma! Wake up, momma! It's a BEAUTIFUL DAY, momma! You're going to miss it! Wake up and enjoy the day, momma!"

And that morning, Punky growled and lifted her paw to beat the positivity out of him.

But THAT morning, Stinky reeled around and smacked Punky three times upside her head.

There was a moment when I thought Stinky Butt had breathed his last breath. The Dirty Harry look in Punky's eye, the one I could see through my hands covering my face, caused all of us, including ninety-pound Lobo, to hold our breath in anticipation of the wrath that was about to be unleashed all over the sweet six-month old kitten I had bottle-fed and raised as my own.

But, Stinky didn't waiver. He smacked her three times in the head, looked her dead in the eye and said, "How about you stop being a little bitch and enjoy the day, too, ok Princess?"

Pierre, who then requested that I stop calling him Stinky Butt, spent the rest of the day enjoying his new reign as king of the house. Punky spent the day in the basement waiting for permission from Pierre to come back upstairs. She wouldn't have to wait long.

A few days after his glorious claim to the throne, Pierre went to do his part to fight kitten overpopulation and get himself fixed. I suppose it is unfair to suggest that he went voluntarily. Or willingly. It was actually a bit of a struggle because his dead silence the whole way there was worse than if he had meowed the whole way. He knew something was up, and he knew he wasn't going to like it. I tried to stay positive and assured him that all would be fine. He would go to sleep, they would give him some great drugs while he was asleep, and he would wake up feeling no pain. If only I had known how right I was.

Pierre's short-lived reign came to a screeching halt the moment he re-entered the house sans boy-parts and highly medicated. Is it wrong to giggle at a drugged kitten? It felt wrong, but also inevitable.

Pierre's trip to do his part to end pet overpopulation also resulted in a large chunk being removed from his shoulder. An abscess required the removal of infected tissue and the insertion of a drain tube. My little Pierre came home to me wrapped in special blue surgical wrap and wearing the cone of shame. I was given medications and instructions to have the drain tube removed the following week. The wound would need to be cleaned regularly and rewrapped. I could handle that. I had successfully raised two boys without excessive hospital visits. I could care for a kitten with a tiny little wound.

So, have any of you actually tried to apply surgical wrap to a six-month old kitten? Yeah.

First, Pierre spent the thirty-minute ride home performing the most impressive acrobatic moves I had ever seen in an attempt to remove the cone of shame. No doubt he anticipated the intense bullying he would encounter if Punky saw him in the thing. He was unsuccessful in removing the cone. He was highly successful, however, in removing his drain tube. Nice. Well, I could just scratch that little chore off my list. Helpful.

Once home, Pierre was clearly not anxious to emerge from the carrier, as we could all hear Punky snickering in the background. Oh yes. Sweet revenge. Damon and I coaxed him out with a few of his favorite cat treats. We then placed him gently on the back of the couch, his favorite resting spot. When he slowly began to slide off the front of the couch, we realized that he was in no condition to be left unattended.

Punky was no longer snickering, but was rolling hysterically on the floor at this point. Gracie was trying to figure out who the heck we had brought home and where the heck her baby Pierre was. Lobo and Lucky were just a little too interested in sniffing Pierre's butt. And the kitten that used to purr non-stop was no longer purring. They had broken his purr! So, the boys and I took turns cradling him protectively and shooing various animals away, mostly Punky.

The next morning I needed to administer his meds and clean his wound. He weighed all of four pounds and I had vaccinated him by myself, so I wasn't the least bit concerned about this. How naive.

I mixed the antibiotic, pulled the appropriate amount into the dropper and turned to Pierre. He looked at me with skepticism and said,

"You really think this is going to be easy, don't you? Ok. Well, despite what is about to occur, remember that I do love you."

I gently cupped his face and began to squeeze the medicine into his mouth. It was the same antibiotic that my kids used to beg for as children (a few times I think they may have made themselves sick on purpose so they could get a prescription for it), so surely Pierre would love it. Right. After I managed to tear his claws out of my left arm, I grabbed a towel to stop the bleeding. I was pretty sure I got some of the medicine in his mouth, at least. He may have even swallowed some of it.

With the bleeding stopped and gauze applied to my wounds, it was time to clean his wound. I managed to get the wrap off and cleanse the area before Pierre flipped out and went for my right arm. I was too quick for him and managed to juke him before he actually made contact. I snatched his wiry little body up again and cradled him in a pseudo-sleeper hold. I then handed the wrap to Damon while I held the clean gauze in place.

Thirty-eight minutes later, we sat Pierre on the floor. Have you ever seen a mummy in real life? Ok, probably not. I don't think they're that common. I mean, you've seen them in movies and books, though, right? Brendan Fraser? So, yeah, that's what was standing before me when I put Pierre on the floor. A scrawny little feline mummy.

Pierre stood there motionless for a moment … and then slowly fell over. We picked him up and placed him back on his feet. He took two steps and then slowly fell over again.

Punky could barely breathe at this point from laughing so hard. She actually had to leave the room to regain her composure.

We unwrapped him and tried again. Twenty two minutes later…you know, it's really best for wounds to breathe a bit.

10 Lady Cujo

So, Lucky's time with us went by quickly. Despite my boot camp efforts, he didn't seem to manage to drop any weight during his time here. He did manage to worm his way into the heart of almost everyone in my home. There are few fosters that my youngest son will allow himself to get attached to. He learned quickly to maintain some level of emotional distance from our temporary companions. One can only have their heart broken but so many times before they learn to establish boundaries. Lucky was one that none of us could help falling for. Each of us has, on several occasions since his adoption, spent time reflecting on how much we miss him. I've even found Lobo appearing to search the house for him.

Still, I was excited to see him find such a perfect family and forever home. It was a wonderful home where I was certain he would live a long, happy life and wouldn't give me a second thought. This turned out to be true. I still see him once or twice a year when his mom brings him to an event, and he shows little excitement to see me. I'm not dead sure he even remembers me. But he's happy and that's all that matters.

I would return to the pound to continue my work. This was how I spent every depressing Thursday at that time, walking through the pound and taking pictures of dogs I desperately want to save and cats that I will probably never be able to save. I would spend hours editing and uploading photos, noting pen numbers and any available information under each photo. I would then spend the next several days responding to questions that I just didn't have the answers to. It was an exhausting and time-consuming process, but I believe it helps save lives.

Still, animal rescuers recognize that one animal may eventually come along that you just cannot save. If you're like me, you simply don't acknowledge the possibility. You just keep taking in fosters with a sort of blind faith that they will find their happily ever after as a result of your work. My next foster would be a perfect example of that.

Her name was Lady. She was a small Boston Terrier that had been surrendered by her people and wasn't doing well in the pound. It was Friday and the pound was full. An owner-surrender who was cowering at the back of her kennel would be among the first to be euthanized. Obviously, I couldn't just let that happen. Unfortunately, I was unable to get her until Sunday, and by then, it would be too late. Our board president and her husband agreed to pull Lady that Friday and hold her for me until Sunday.

After an anxious weekend, I arrived at headquarters Sunday afternoon to pick Lady up from Steve and Bobbi. Since they had pulled her on Friday, Lady had spent the weekend cowering in the back of her crate in their kennel area and growling at anyone who came near her. They warned me that she was very aggressive and that she had refused to leave her crate all weekend. As we stood by her carrier discussing our concerns, she stared and growled at me. When Steve put his fingers to her carrier, she lunged at him in Cujo fashion.

What would we do if I couldn't socialize her? Do we take her back to the pound? Do we euthanize her? We obviously couldn't adopt her out, and I couldn't subject my family to such a vicious animal in my home indefinitely. How long should we give her? We eventually agreed that I would give her three days to show any sign of being rehabilitatable. If she continued to be this aggressive, we would simply have no options for her. It would be a heart wrenching decision, and it would have to be mine.

A quick internal pep talk, and I gingerly took the carrier to my car, looking very much like Jeremy Renner in the Hurt Locker and using my sweet voice to try to reassure Lady. Please note that my sweet voice is reserved for animals. People do not get my sweet voice. Unless you have cookies. Or Doritos.

I slipped a few treats into her carrier because I am not above buying someone's love and then quietly closed the car door. We drove home in silence, partly because I didn't want to overwhelm her and partly because I was busy worrying. How am I going to do this? What if she bites one of my children? What if I can't keep her? How do I take a dog to the pound? I can't return her to the pound. I will have to spend hours working with her to get her to trust me. How will I get my other work done? What if I get fired? Will my animals think that I don't love them if I'm spending all of my time with her? What if one of the cats slips through the door into the basement when I'm not looking? What if she has to be euthanized? I can't take a perfectly healthy young dog to be euthanized.

This was the running dialogue in my head the entire thirty-minute drive home. I finally pulled into my driveway and tried to think of a plan. When nothing brilliant came to mind, I decided to just go with my gut.

I walked her carrier into the basement and set it down. I put some food and water in her bowls and then sat down by her carrier. To my surprise, she came to the front of the carrier and looked at me curiously. She wasn't growling. In fact, she looked like she wanted to come see me. Although I couldn't be entirely sure that this wasn't just a ploy for her to get close enough to my face to bite it off, I opened the carrier door anyway. And at that very moment, this vicious, terrified, aggressive dog turned into the sweetest, happiest little girl alive.

As the veil of anxiety was lifted, little Lady began to explore her surroundings. Tail wagging, she walked the perimeter of the room to be sure all was safe. Then, she trotted back to where I was sitting, climbed into my lap, and began to kiss my face. She was safe and grateful.

I had given her three days. It took her three minutes.

11 THIS WAS GOING TO BE A TOUGH ONE

Depriving a dog of food, and more importantly, treats, is always a risky move.

On the morning a few weeks after coming to stay with me, little Lady went for her spay surgery. As such, she couldn't have breakfast or her regular morning treat the day of her surgery. Now, since no one else in the house was getting spayed that morning, the rest of us still had our treats. Punky got her can of wet cat food. Stinky Butt got his organic cat treats and Gracie got her Temptations. Lobo got his chew. The boys got their Pop Tarts (still not sure those really qualify as treats, but whatever). I had my pot of coffee.

As we all sat enjoying our treats just like any other day, Lady sat looking at each of us, dumbfounded.

"I don't want to sound unappreciative, what with you rescuing me from the pound and all. But what, exactly, is going on here? I'm sorry, but I don't understand what's happening. Why does…Where is my…hmm."

She tried just clearing her throat a few times. When I went to the kitchen for a coffee refill, she tried to guide me to the treat cabinet instead. She tried getting right up in my face and hypnotizing me with her sad Boston Terrier eyes. When that didn't work, she simply walked away, disgusted. Of course, it didn't occur to me to follow her. Lady was decidedly perturbed. So, she did what any self-respecting dog would do in this situation…

She went to the litter box. She found her own "treats." And not only did she get her own "treats" from the litter box, but she spread them all over my carpet and dissertation research which the cats had conveniently strewn about my office.

As though I wasn't already struggling to motivate myself to finish my literature review, now I had the added bonus of smelling cat poo while I studied.

"Lady! What were you thinking???"

Lady initially looked at me with remorseful eyes. Then she looked at Lobo napping peacefully with a full belly. The indignation quickly returned to her and she said,

"I think the more important question here is what were YOU thinking?"

Well, she had a point. Still, this had to happen so I cleaned up the mess and then loaded her into her carrier.

"Whoa. Wait a second. What is THIS? You're taking me back? It was only a little cat poo! I'm sorry! It won't happen again! I don't need treats. I don't need breakfast. I'll just clean the crumbs up off the floor. See? That will be good for both of us. I get food and you get a clean floor! Please don't take me back!"

Oh yes, she was going to be a difficult one to part with. You do fall in love with each of them. But there's something about the emotionally broken ones that dig at your heart a bit more. I tried to assure her that she was not going back to the pound, but she wouldn't listen. She knew wherever she was going, it wasn't a happy place, and she was quickly losing hope.

Little Lady was so good at the vet's office as we waited for them to take her back where she would wait for her spay surgery. But what I saw when I picked her up afterward explained so clearly how fragile she was. I would need to spend the rest of my time with her continuing to build her self-esteem, because her previous experiences had left her with almost none.

Really, when I think about it, I am shocked that any being can survive being handed over to a facility that can provide them only limited care and compassion; where they live their days behind bars; where their days are numbered, literally. The ones that wag their tail happily from behind the kennel door have an understanding of where they are and know that they must win over one of the few people who walk through if they ever hope to make it out alive. Little Lady was not one of those dogs. In the pound, she cowered nervously at the back of her kennel, looking up with worrisome little eyes. She wasn't trying.

Consequently, a trip to the vet for her was much more devastating than it is for the average young dog. When I arrived to pick her up and the vet tech brought her out to the waiting room to me, Lady looked as devastated as she had when I first met her at the pound. She clearly thought someone had given up on her…again. Her entire body told the story. Her tail was tucked, head down, and her tiny little legs moved reluctantly as the tech coaxed her around the corner towards me.

She didn't recognize me initially and really seemed entirely uninterested in anything going on around her. She was simply doing whatever she was told to do with no desire left in her to fight it. After she approached me cautiously and sniffed my leg, her ears perked up, her tail wagged, and she looked up at me with excited eyes and exclaimed, "You really came back for me!"

Yeah, I held it together in the vet's office. But when I got Lady into the car, it hit me just how much this one is going to break my heart to part with. I did part with her, because tomorrow brings another weekly trip to the pound where there are more babies waiting to be saved. It involved two boxes of tissues. She went to live with a family that already had other small dogs that Lady seemed to quickly take to. She was a far more confident dog now, and she didn't appear even a little bit worried as I left her with her new family. I, however, was devastated. As wonderful as the family was that she was leaving me for, she took a little piece of me with her.

12 HOW I BECAME A THREE-A-DAY RUNNER

With Lady safely in her new home, I shifted to taking in a few foster cats. Cats are more challenging for me to foster, because they are harder to find good homes for. There is little demand in the South for cats, and really, if you want a cat, you need look no farther than your local dump. Check out behind the grocery store. Hell, take a look under your porch. They're everywhere around here. Honestly, people. Spay and neuter. TNR. These are simple and inexpensive ways to save lives.

Anyway, I took in two new foster cats. Now, I believe there is a small streak of crazy in every animal rescuer. Ok, maybe some of us have a bigger crazy streak than others. One fall night it became very clear that the animals were stealing my sanity and that my streak of crazy was ever-increasing. It was 8pm and I had just finished up my 3rd run of the day. Why three runs do you ask? Am I so dedicated to my health, fitness, or sport that I have moved from simple 2-a-days to 3-a-days? Am I planning to run some super crazy British Special Forces designed run, thus requiring extra training? Well, yeah, but that wasn't the reason for the 3rd run that day.

I ran my 3rd run of the day, well after dark, in my mismatched pajamas and a pair of slippers because I locked myself out of the house. I locked myself out of the house because I am in the habit of locking doors automatically since my time working in prison and in the habit of closing doors immediately behind me since the multiple escapes of nearly every cat in my home. The only beings left in the house were a very panicked Lobo, a mildly concerned Gracie, a delighted Pierre (who thought I was playing some sort of game), and a smirking Punky. I swear that little b-word rolled her eyes at me. My new foster cats Barney and Sidney were in the basement, and so were unaware of my plight or I believe Barney would have opened the door to let me back in. I firmly believed it was in his power to do that.

At any rate, the animals were clearly not going to let me back in. I fully admit that it actually took me a moment to process this. The boys were house-sitting for my parents who lived a mile up the road; a long, dark, creature-infested, wooded road. Chupacabra-infested, and I suspect even a few Bigfoots. (Did you know that the plural of Bigfoot is Bigfoots? Learned that little piece of trivia on Animal Planet's "Finding Bigfoot." An excellent show. Very sound research practices. Plus, entirely entertaining.)

Still, I needed to get to my children in order to regain entry into my home. I might have considered asking my neighbor across the street to drive me over, but she wasn't home from work yet. I considered walking up the road a bit to another neighbor's house, but then thought, "Hey! What's the point of being a runner if I don't use the skill in an emergency?" Yeah, because apparently I'm in training for the apocalypse, and running is going to be the thing that saves me. (At the time I originally wrote this, that was sarcasm. I have since realized that this actually IS how I'm going to survive the zombie apocalypse in the future, and now I'm just a little offended that I would ever joke about this.)

I opted to take off my robe and leave it on the porch railing, because it would look odd to go running down the road in my robe. Really, my thought process here was that running down the road in a robe was too Hitchhiker's Guide and might send passersby into a panic and grabbing their towels. Best not to set off that series of events. (If you don't get the reference, you should probably be reading more high-quality books. But first, finish this one. I'm delightfully entertaining and I have important things to say.)

So, off I went, and I must say the first half mile wasn't too bad. It was a gorgeous night out. It was cool, but comfortable, and there was just enough moonlight to allow me to see where I was going. I was really starting to enjoy myself and thinking how great this run would be if only I were wearing sneakers, and running pants, and a running shirt, and a running bra.

However, this is the point where things started to go horribly wrong.

First, a car came. Some may have considered that good luck and attempted to waive the driver down and ask for a ride, but when you spend your days watching Criminal Minds and teaching criminal justice, your gut reaction is to dive into the nearest row of trees far off the road and out of sight of the oncoming serial killer (because clearly a road that dead ends into the lake is the obvious place for a serial killer to be out for an evening drive). Right, well while the moon was bright enough to allow me to see where I was going, it was not bright enough to allow me to see the pile of leaves and bushes that I was diving into. It was not bright enough for me to see whatever very large animal was lingering and rustling ever so slightly in the woods to my left. It was not bright enough for me to identify the gooey substance under my hand when I pushed myself back up. Coincidentally, this row of trees was in the same approximate area where Lucky lured me into the jungle spider web last summer. Yeah, I did my dance after getting back to my feet. Then I set off again.

Second, I'm not nineteen anymore. Running in slippers is ill-advised. (Really, I shouldn't blame age for that one. Running in slippers is always ill-advised. At any age. It's just, at nineteen I was probably too unfocused to realize it.) Just after the unfortunate tree-diving incident when I started back on my run, my slippers began to give way. They wouldn't stay on my feet unless I scrunched my toes up inside them. Another quarter-mile and the shooting pains up my shins and down my neck and shoulders told me this was a bad idea. I'm pretty sure I heard my left shoulder call me old. My legs begged me to stop, so I did. Besides, there was no reason for me to be in a hurry. It's not like anyone was going to see me since I was now on a side road that very few people drive down. No one was going to see me, except for that person looking out of his window.

Third, even if you move from a run to a walk, the neighbors are still going to stare out their window at you walking down the street in your mismatched jammies and pair of slippers while dialing what looked like only 3 numbers on their phone.

Never fear, though. All's well that ends well. I made it to my parents' house where my son rescued me from my peril, drove me back home, and let me back into my house. It was at that point that he asked why I hadn't just used a neighbor's phone to call him.

Cause I'm a runner. That's why.

(Totally worth it just to say that line.)

13 CALL ME (SMILEY FACE)

The newest foster cats were fitting in quite well in my home, but it wasn't long before Sidney went on to live in a wonderful forever home. Her new family provides updates from time to time, letting us know how very much in love they are with her. That left Barney behind to establish a new friendship with one of the long-timers. It would appear that Stinky Butt Pierre was his choice and Stinky quickly decided that his new best friend Barney was not going anywhere.

That posed a bit of a problem for me. I keep a box of tissues in my car to wipe away the tears I cry with every foster that gets adopted. I have actually gotten much better about that over time. I cry much less over the dogs that go, but the cats remain an issue for me. Cats, in general, seem to hold less value in our society than dogs. I always fear that they will not be cuddled and cared for in their new homes the way dogs are. It is a somewhat irrational fear since I take great care to ensure that each of my foster animals go on to the perfect homes for them and that their new families are worthy. Still, it is always a little sadder to see the cats go. The bottom line is that I am ok with breaking my own heart every few months as I watch my sweet foster babies move onto the next chapter in their life.

My problem with Barney and Stinky's new-found friendship was that I was not only breaking my own heart by allowing Barney to be adopted. I now had to worry about how Stinky would handle losing the one who he had decided was his best friend in the whole world.

Still, I couldn't have another foster failure. Punky was unlikely to find a home with her, well, let's call them eccentricities, and Stinky was becoming increasingly stinky and also unlikely to ever leave my home. Apparently people prefer their cats not to smell horrifically bad. Several vet visits and extensive testing has left his condition undiagnosed. All we knew is that he often had painful mouth ulcers and his saliva was filled with bacteria. When he tries to groom himself, he simply spreads the bacteria all over his body, making himself dirtier and smellier. Steroids and antibiotics worked in the short term, but the condition always comes back. I would eventually make the decision to adopt both Stinky and Punky, foster failures number two and three. I could not have a fourth cat as a foster failure.

This may not have been so much of an issue while my children were still in high school and living at home. It seems to be slightly more acceptable to have a house full of cats when you also have a very busy life outside of them. Children indicate that you have some type of human social life. Or that you did, at some point in your life, anyway. However, that house full of cats quickly translates into sad and crazy once the children move out and you are no longer quite so busy outside of the home. The bottom line is that you can't keep every one you fall in love with and you can't keep every one that your other pets fall in love with. Sometimes fostering simply breaks your heart.

When Mindy sent me the text message "Can you please call me?" with a little smiley face at the end, I knew it wasn't going to be great news. Well, at least not great for me.

Barney was, quite possibly, the coolest, most laid back, most loving being I had ever encountered. Anytime Punky smacked him because he had the nerve to exist in her world, usually several times a day, he always responded with a mix of hurt and surprise. He would back up a few inches to give her space, but never fought back. Of course, he didn't run away and hide, either. He just accepted her for all of her drama.

He also spent his days walking around the house chatting with everyone just checking in to see how their day was going. If you sat still long enough, he would come up and give you a hug. Punky, of course, was excluded from this practice. Lobo was not. Barney was a cuddler and he cuddled his way into my heart before I even brought him into my home.

When I returned Mindy's call and she said she had a potential adopter for him, I had a near panic attack. I broke the news to my kids and little Stinky Butt. I consulted with Punky briefly, hoping she might help me teach him some bad habits quickly so this family wouldn't want him. She just smirked and walked away. Ungrateful B-word. I thought maybe I could teach him on my own, but Barney just responded to my hissing and growling with a "You look like you could use a hug, lady. You ok? Here, let me give you a hug. Hugs make it all better."

The next day I reluctantly packed him up and drove him to headquarters to meet the potential adopters. After getting him to headquarters, I realized I had forgotten my wallet that I would need to buy dinner, so I drove back home to get it. My mom happened to stop by when I got home. While standing in my hallway at home talking to my mom, Mindy called to tell me the adopters were already there and had quickly made their decision. Barney was the obvious choice, as I knew he would be.

I wasn't there to hug him and say goodbye. I had just dropped him off and left him, and it would take me at least thirty minutes to get back.

I told Mindy to tell him I loved him and that he hadn't done anything wrong, and then I broke down. I don't care how perfect the adoptive family is, there is always a concern that your sweet foster baby might think, even for a second, that they did something wrong to make you not want them anymore. Determined to get back in time to hug him and tell him this myself, I jumped into the car and sped my way back to headquarters.

God bless his new family for waiting for me to get there before taking him out of my life. I hugged him and told him how much I loved him. I briefly considered just darting out the door with him clutched in my arms, but I decided to be a grown up and reminded myself of why I do what I do. I put him down and watched him walk quietly into his carrier and tell his family he was ready to go home. I knew then that he was going to be just fine.

Sometimes fostering breaks your heart, but I think every time it breaks, it heals back a little stronger so you can give a little more love to the next baby in need.

14 WE'RE CLEAR ON THE NOT TOUCHING PART?

During the short time that I've been fostering, I've always had exceptional luck winning over the animals that I bring into my home. Even the terrified and snarly Lady melted into the most loving little girl I'd ever met as soon as I got her home. Her forever family will tell you that she loves nothing more than to give kisses now.

When I brought the trembling and terrified Pearl home, though, my luck came to a screeching halt. Pearl was abandoned by her family, dumped at the pound on a day when the pound was set to euthanize several dogs. As a dog surrendered by her owner, she likely would have been one of them. Thankfully, because the pound called asking for our help, Pearl was among the 8 dogs that were rescued that day and none had to be euthanized.

It was not hard to understand why this little girl was so reluctant to trust me, the strange woman with a house full of teenagers and the nerve to put a leash on her and take her outside to go potty. Pearl had clearly never been on a leash before. That was enough for her to quickly decide that I would not earn her trust so easily.

Naturally, I turned to our veterinarian for advice on how to build some trust with Pearl. It killed me that she didn't adore me the way my other fosters had. Lexi's advice involved me getting on my hands and knees, yawning "audibly" (which I interpreted as "make obnoxiously loud seizure sounds") and smacking my lips a lot. Really, Lexi? Because the constant air of cat litter and dog poo that I carry around with me everywhere I go is not enough humiliation? Because I am not already destined to live a life alone with a house full of cats? Because I don't already make an idiot of myself on a consistent basis? Really???

Fine.

I came home and spent several hours over the next few days kneeling in front of Pearl's crate, yawning loudly, and smacking my lips a lot. Has anyone else in the entire world ever won a dog over with this behavior? And where are all of the YouTube videos of people doing this, because I know I looked like a straight idiot. Someone should have been pointing at me and ridiculing me while I did this. Luckily none of my neighbors opted to pay me a surprise visit during these episodes. I call them episodes because I'm quite certain that I looked and sounded like I was having some sort of fit.

Admittedly, Pearl stopped trembling when I did this. What she did instead was look at me with a mix of incredulity and pity. Occasionally she would wag her tail. When I went to pet her in response, she backed up into the corner saying,

"Whoa there. I didn't mean you could touch me. That was just a pity wag. You just look so sad. But for real I'm going to need you to back up out of my crate."

Eventually, Pearl and I came to an understanding. I would make sure she had food and water and plenty of clean blankets, all without actually touching her. She would wag her tail at me in response, but she was very clear on the "me not touching her" part.

Still, how was I supposed to get a dog adopted when she wouldn't even let me touch her? Ummmm, yeah. I've got this dog here. She's real cute. You just can't ever, uh, touch her. Right. But, still, I guess if the Gremlins salesman managed to get those ugly little things adopted with all of their warning labels, then surely I could convince someone to take this cute little untouchable Chihuahua.

First applicants. Only applicants, actually. The first and only applicants to express interest in this girl called to set up a time to meet her. I explained timidly that she was the sweetest little thing, but she just had this little problem with touch. They were undeterred. It was a married couple and when they arrived for their visit, I led them into the living room where Pearl's crate was set up. The wife immediately sat on the floor in front of her crate while the husband and I allowed them some space. Pearl didn't necessarily come out right away when her potential new mom gently opened her crate, but she did come out. Eventually. And crawled into her mom's lap. And spent the rest of the family's visit contentedly cuddled in the woman's arms. Apparently, the no-touching rule only applied to me. She wasn't meant to bond with me. I wasn't her person. I was just her means of getting to the place she belonged. She was selective. And that was ok. It was clear she had chosen her new family, and I couldn't have been happier for this fragile girl. Pearl left shortly after that to go to her forever home for cuddles and love by the fire and a cozy bed next to her new fur-sister. I got to try to regain some of the dignity I had lost over the few weeks she was with me.

15 FLASHES OF ORANGE AND BLOOD-COVERED WALLS

Punky had been with me a full year by this point, so it was time for her to visit the vet. She needed her vaccinations updated and her microchip implanted. All of this involved sticking sharp objects into her skin. Now, if it's not already clear, Punky can be a bit … temperamental. She likes her life to be comfortable, and she is willing to do whatever it takes to ensure that it stays comfortable. I figured that the vet's chance of making it out of the room alive after trying to vaccinate this beautiful girl was about fifty-fifty. I figured my odds were slightly better if I were just willing to feign shock at the vet's actions and let her take the fall. I just wasn't sure how this whole scenario was going to play out.

Oddly enough, it started out well. Punky went willingly into the cat carrier without protest. She did look up at me with worried eyes and meowed softly during the short drive to the vet's office. Once inside the examination room, she continued to look quite timid and worried. I kind of started to feel sorry for the poor girl. She seemed almost vulnerable. Poor Punky.

Then memories of Punky beating the crap out of my Stinky Butt Pierre flashed through my mind, and I snapped out of it. This was clearly a tactic to lull us all into a false sense of security so she could inflict the most damage when she decided to strike. I urged the extremely young and tiny vet tech not to be fooled. This beautiful, sweet cat would turn on anyone and everyone without warning. I told her stories of ceiling tile horrors and unprovoked face attacks. (She liked to hide in the basement ceiling tiles IT style until someone unwittingly stuck their head up through one of them looking for her and then she'd latch on like a shrieking, claw-covered leach.) Admittedly, these unfortunate events were prompted by the addition of new fosters into what she has claimed as HER home, but I felt it best to make her sound nearly feral to insure the utmost precaution on the part of the vet staff.

Clearly my stories made an impression, because I heard mumbled voices outside the room as the tech consulted with the vet, and several minutes later the vet walked hesitantly into the room avoiding eye contact with Punky and speaking in hushed tones. Determined to do her job, however, she approached Punky and began to pet her. Assured by Punky's docile response, the vet began to examine her. Dear lord, she even put her fingers in Punky's mouth, a certain death move, but Punky was unfazed.

Reassured by a calm Punky, the vet proceeded to administer Punky's rabies vaccination. Still nothing. Now further emboldened, the vet pulled out the microchip. Well, this is where it all gets a bit fuzzy for me. I remember the vet asking me to turn Punky around so her head (and teeth and front claws) were facing away from her and toward me. I recall some hissing that quickly evolved into a gurgly growling sound that I'm certain no other human has ever heard and survived to tell about it. I remember flashes of orange darting around the room and shooting pains in my hands and arms. I remember saying something to the effect of "Good gracious woman! Who cares if the chip scans! Just put her back in the carrier, and give me something to stop the bleeding!"

The good news is that all of my open wounds healed within a month or so. The bad news is that I will have to administer future vaccinations myself. So, yeah, I'm taking volunteers to hold her head (and teeth and front claws) away from me while I stick the needle in because that seems to be the position of greatest vulnerability. I'm pretty sure I'm not allowed back to the vet's office. Ever.

16 No Response

Some of the joys of fostering lie in the utter ridiculousness that living creatures exhibit at times. I think my favorite part of fostering is getting to know the various quirks and neuroses that each different foster animal brings into my home.

My sweet little foster baby Emma, known in my house as Emmy Lou Who, really seemed to love other animals. All of the animals. But I think she may have love them a little too much.

Since she was pregnant when I brought her home from the pound, VERY pregnant, and I didn't know her medical history, I wouldn't allow Lobo or any of the cats to go into the basement where her crate was. While we waited patiently (well, some of us waited not so patiently), Emmy seemed content to ignore the animals that would peer in at her from the basement door. She had bigger issues to concern herself with, like how she would ever get her figure back after giving birth to puppies that were clearly part Sasquatch.

I was a nervous wreck, but also really excited to experience the miracle of birth. I mean, I'd already experienced the miracle twice when making my own two Sasquatch babies, but those experiences were very unmiraculous in the moment. Childbirth when you're the one doing the actual birthing is really just a test of wills to see who is more stubborn, you or your two weeks overdue monster baby. I wanted to experience the miracle when someone else was dealing with the pain, and I could just watch in awe while eating Doritos and enjoying a beer.

The waiting was tedious. I didn't leave the basement for four days, and I didn't sleep for four nights. I ate my meals on the couch next to her crate. I did my work on the couch next to her crate. I'm not entirely sure I even showered during that time. Sometimes she would come out and cuddle with me on the couch and I could feel the puppies move inside her swollen belly. Aside from my own children, I hadn't experienced childbirth, and that doesn't really count since I didn't actually see anything. I just felt the pain that makes you want to reach into someone's throat and pull out their esophagus with your bare hand. I was determined to watch these babies being born. I took Emmy's temperature regularly to try to predict the onset of labor. I'm certain this only served to make her more uncomfortable, though she never protested or complained. I worried other more experienced volunteers with questions about what to do if one of the puppies got stuck or if Emmy refused to nurse them or if a tornado hit in the middle of the birthing process or if a chupacabra snuck in and stole one of the puppies when I wasn't looking. It was a long process and a lot of really frightening scenarios made their way into my head.

Emmy and I were in a standoff. When I pulled her from the pound, everyone said she was about to go any minute. I anticipated her giving birth in her carrier on the drive home from the pound. I continued to anticipate her giving birth every second of every minute of the next four days. I refused to sleep for fear I would miss the blessed event. How I managed to stay mostly awake for four days is beyond me, but four days was clearly my limit. In my twenties I could stay awake for days without the slightest bit of fatigue, but in my thirties, I was not as resilient as I used to be. I needed my sleep, desperately.

Around midnight of the fourth day, I fell asleep on the couch next to Emmy's crate. Actually, I probably did more than fall asleep. I passed out next to Emmy's crate. I was dead to the world. Clearly no sound was penetrating my slumbering brain because the sound of a Chihuahua giving birth to multiple Sasquatch puppies wasn't enough to wake me. At 6am the next morning, I awoke to Emmy cleaning her three newborn puppies. I had missed all of it.

My disappointment at missing their birth was short-lived. I looked at those tiny little puppies and melted. In fairness, only two of them were tiny. One was rather large, twice the size of the smallest little one, but the smallest one was so small that she was barely moving. She was barely breathing. She was barely eating. I put her close to Emmy and encouraged her to eat, but she didn't. I rubbed her back a bit and place her mouth up to one of Emmy's nipples. Nothing. I picked her up and held her between my palms, trying to warm her and massage some life into her. No response. No response…

I cuddled her and prayed over her and begged her to live. I carried her around in arms trying, refusing to believe that I didn't have the power to make her ok. If I just held her long enough, she'd get warm, and she'd start breathing again.

But she didn't.

She couldn't.

This tiny, fragile, beautiful brown puppy took her last few, weak breaths in my hands while her momma nursed her brothers. I just sat there for a while cradling her little lifeless body willing her to take another breath. Begging. Crying. Sobbing. Raging.

But she wouldn't.

She was gone.

Gone to the Bridge after only a few hours of life.

I named her Julia.

And I then buried her near the Cattyshack in my backyard.

***

Thankfully, the two male puppies thrived. I named them Victor (Hugo) and Leo (Tolstoy) because I was going through some sort of phase where I thought I was all literary and educated. In fairness, I love Victor Hugo. But I've never even read Tolstoy. Hell, I can't even tell you what he's written. Anna Karenina, maybe? Wait. I read that. I mean, not all of it because there are a crap ton of Russian names to keep track of in that book, and they all, for real, look exactly the same to my ethnocentric American eyes. If anyone ever dumbs it down into a book with American sounding names (or at least, like, British sounding names), then I'll dive right back in. I feel like it was probably a solid storyline that I just couldn't follow, being too distracted by all the 'skis'.

After the babies came, however, my little Emmy Lou Who made it known in no uncertain terms that she was entirely aware that there was a house full of animals that she did not have access to. She would talk, in a very animated manner, to the raccoons that knock over the trash cans and to the birds that build their nests under the upper deck, just outside the basement door. When my Lobo would peer in at her through the basement window, Emmy would lose her ever-loving mind.

Eventually, I relented and allowed Lobo into the basement to visit with Emmy, thinking there was a strong possibility that she may try to eat him. I just wanted her to calm down and see that he was not a threat to her or her babies. I did not, however, expect her to be so gleefully excited about finally meeting him that she would actually pee with joy. Yes, this little girl peed right where she stood when that giant of a bear came into the basement. Then she began playing.

After that, I found that Emmy doesn't just love dogs. She also loves cats (and the cats were super-excited about that...).

So, once she'd safely met Lobo, I gave her free roam of the house on a regular basis. She still spent most of her time in the basement with her babies, but occasionally she would come upstairs for some Emmy Time. When she came upstairs, she spent a full five minutes prancing excitedly in place like it was Christmas morning, and she was looking at a tree full of presents with her name on them. When she finally regained her composure, she spent several more minutes going from animal to animal saying,

"Hi! Hi! I'm Emma! Hi! I remember you! You're a cat! I love cats! I'm a dog! My name is Emma! You can call me Emmy! Hi! Hi! Hi! Hi! Hi! Hi! Wanna play?"

No, Emma. No, the cats don't want to play. They want me to give you a sedative.

Eventually, after she made her rounds to greet Lobo and all the cats, she would find a suitable lap to cuddle in. Now, it didn't really matter if there was already a computer or a book orrrrr a cat in that lap. Emmy managed to plop her cute little behind right down on top of who or whatever might already be there, and there she would stay for as long as she thought she could leave her babies alone.

17 ALCATRAZ

It felt good, saving so many lives. Every time I would pull a dog from the pound and bring them home, it warmed my heart. I could walk through the pound and know that I had saved several lives, one at a time, by opening my home to these dogs. Yet, it wasn't as satisfying as it should have been, because I had walked into the cat room every week for two years and had yet to save a single cat from there. Most of the cats I photographed each week died there, in the pound, all alone. Obviously, I had fostered cats. I had fostered several cats. The problem was that we were constantly bombarded by local community members bringing us cats and kittens needing homes and so few homes willing to adopt a cat or a kitten. A dog may spend a few months in foster care, where a cat may spend years.

I needed to feel better about this. I needed to be able to pull some cats from the pound and not just one or two, but many. I wanted to save some feline lives. So, one afternoon I was standing in my driveway talking to my parents, talking about how ridiculously thick the grass was and how difficult it was to keep mowed. Yeah, maybe I whine a little too much. Anyway, I naturally transitioned into talking about cats (totally natural transition … I can transition any conversation into talking about cats) and mentioning that someday I would like to build a cattery in the backyard so I could foster more.

The following week, my dad showed up with some lumber and a posthole digger. (Seriously. Let that sink in. I made some passing comment about a wish I had, and the next week this man was making it happen. THIS is why I am still single. Unreasonable expectations. Well, that and my desperate need for independence, my inability to share my space, and my low tolerance for drama.) For the last few months of summer, he and my sons spent every weekend and many weekdays digging holes, measuring posts, sawing pieces of wood, hammering nails, and unrolling fencing.

Sweat. There was a lot of sweat. Lobo helped where he could, carrying around the large tree branches the boys had cut out of the way so the cattery could go up.

"We gonna keep more foster dogs out here, mom?" Lobo mumble around the tree hanging out of his large jaws.

"It's for cats, Lobo. We're gonna save lots more cats."

"Cats? Oh. OK." Yeah, there was a hint of disappointment in his voice as he moped away to the other side of the yard and sat down to chew on his tree.

The project took several weeks to complete, but the finished project was beautiful. The cattery itself matched my house. It had three little windows and a roofed front porch with a little loft area inside where the porch extended out from the house. My dad installed lots of shelving inside so the cats would have plenty of areas to climb and play. We painted the floor a deep red that would be easy to sweep and mop. We painted the walls a cream color, and my dad installed extra screening on the windows so we wouldn't have any escapees in the middle of the night.

The outdoor fencing was complete so the cats would have a large front yard to play in along with a partial tree to climb. I furnished the inside with brand new ceramic dishes and fresh, clean litter boxes. I placed a basket of toys on the floor and set up some scratching posts on the porch. I stocked up on Cat Chow, treats, and several bags of litter, as well as bleach and Parvosol to make sure no germies would proliferate. I named it the Cattyshack, but my son's friends called it AlCATraz. They said it looked like a cat prison. Lobo was security and I was the warden. Whatever. I was excited to bring my first residents home and see what they thought.

After some discussion, we decided on three of the younger cats that were currently living in crates at the humane society headquarters. Manny was a small orange tabby cat that came to us by way of our board vet. A man passing through the area witnessed this tiny seven-week old kitten get hit by a car and left in the road to die. (*sigh* Yeah, no. Just go about your business. It's cool. Just leave a living, breathing life to writhe in pain frightened and alone in the middle of the road until he dies. That's a totally cool way to be a human.)

The actually cool human that rescued Manny picked the tiny, broken kitten up and took him to the closest vet he could find. As luck and God would have it, he drove miles out of his way to the one vet office where our board member happened to be working. She took Manny into surgery to repair a broken pelvis and tail, committing him as one of our foster cats. This little guy was a trooper and he rebounded from his surgery well, becoming a happy, playful kitten full of energy and spirit. By the time he came to stay with me, he was several months old, and unless you looked closely at his crooked tail, you really wouldn't know he'd ever suffered any trauma in his life.

The second resident was a gorgeous Colorpoint Siamese named Laki. He was a charmer, wanting nothing more than to cuddle with whatever human would make a lap for him. He did well with the other cats and loved playing with the toys I'd provided, but he would drop everything whenever one of us entered the Cattyshack. As soon as you would start petting his soft fur, he would begin purring and climb lazily into your lap.

The last resident was a cherubic little ginger named Kisses. She had the roundest little face I'd ever seen, which only grew rounder during her time with me. (She was a big fan of food.) She held her own roughhousing with the boys but was also very much a girl. She was the most independent of the three, ok with attention from visitors, but certainly not prepared to beg for attention the way Laki would. She would, however, light up whenever Lobo would visit. He was definitely her favorite, and she would flirt with him through the fencing as he paced around looking for a good spot to roll around in the grass. This was one of Kisses' favorite things. Lobo would flop down on his back, kick his legs up in the air, and make low grumbly sounds as he wallowed around. And Kisses would laugh and laugh. "Lobo, you're so silly!"

18 Is That Meth? And Do You Want To Adopt A Cat?

On my grading days, I generally spend the day in my robe on the couch with my laptop. Since my tiny neighborhood rarely receives unannounced visitors and my neighbors are accustomed to seeing me in my unkempt states, this generally isn't an issue. One day, however, my tiny neighborhood received some very unannounced visitors. At 11am on this particular morning, as I lounged on the couch in my robe with my laptop on my lap grading criminal justice papers, I heard loud banging across the street. I glanced out the window and saw about ten men in dark clothes carrying what I can only assume were large, powerful automatic weapons emerging from a beat up old van and attempting to enter my neighbor's front door.

My first reaction - close and lock the sliding door.

My second reaction - put on some makeup. Now, hear me out. I mean, I'm a single woman. Keep in mind that my second reaction came after seeing ATF on the back of one of their vests. I would not have responded this way if I thought they were criminals, just so we're clear. You just never know when an eligible young ATF agent is going to come question you about activities across the street, and let me say that eyeliner is not easy to apply when you're hands are shaking in response to a surprise task force takeover of your neighborhood.

My third reaction – call the owner of the home.

Lobo's reaction – haunting, unsettling silence. Not a peep. He just watched. This did not help the shaking.

The cats' reaction - disappear.

Tia, the homeowner, got to my house 15 minutes later parking at the house behind me and crawling through the woods to get here, her large black lab, Rocky, with her.

Lobo's reaction - take out his nervous aggression on Rocky.

The cats' reaction - disappear more.

Luckily, I was able to calm Lobo and get him to smell and recognize his best friend, and he calmed down a bit. Still, now I had two large dogs in my home which were both nervous and anxious about the activity across the road.

I should point out that while Tia still owned the home, she was no longer living there. She was renting the home out to a young couple and apparently eight or ten of their closest relatives. Tia and I spent the next two hours watching agents going in and out of the house while she called everyone she knew to figure out how to get these people evicted from her home. Eventually, we decided it was time to go investigate out in the open instead of peering suspiciously out the windows. Clearly they needed our expert input on the situation. They were all just standing around looking at each other. By this time, Animal Control had also arrived apparently due to the couple's pit bull and min pin, and I needed to know what they were doing with the animals. The plight of the couple's two young children was also a concern, though I admittedly didn't think of them until much later. Besides, the agents had moved the rusted out old van into my driveway, so I felt that gave me cause to be "one of those people."

A few of the deputies spoke to us and told Tia that if it were them, they would be at the Courthouse at that moment to get eviction proceedings started. They assured us both that the concern was not meth production, so at least I could sleep knowing that the entire neighborhood wasn't going to explode.

I did try to get one of the CIU investigators to adopt Rosie, one of our long-time and highly unadoptable dogs. When I asked him if they were taking the animals in the house and explained that my concern was as an animal rescuer, he asked what I had for adoption. I tried to get him to consider one of my many foster cats, but he declined. He then asked if we had any big dogs for adoption. Of course, I said yes and when he asked what we had, my brain froze up. The only thing that came into my head was Lab mixes. We've got Lab mixes. Lots of Lab mixes. (Yeah, I'm pretty sure we didn't have a single Lab mix at that time.) And since I clearly came across as a bumbling idiot, he quickly lost interest in talking to me about animals.

The investigators then wanted to know about the renters and Tia assured them that I knew the most about them since I had the most contact. Yeah. If my brain freezes up over the animals available for adoption, you know my brain froze up over the activities of these suspected drug distributors or arms dealers or sex traffickers. I'm still not entirely sure what was happening over there. I gave them, I am quite sure, absolutely no helpful information. I did try to sound intelligent, though. So that's something.

So, to sum up, my immediate response to any emergent situation is eyeliner. My brain freezes up when asked about adoptable animals during a drug raid. I cannot grade Criminal Justice papers when there is Criminal Justice activity going on outside my door, and apparently I had access to the good stuff right across the street all this time and didn't even know.

And, in case ATF or CIU are reading this, I am just joking about that good stuff comment. You'd know that if you knew me. Excellent work out there that day, men.

I was so happy when Tia said the renters were moving out and she would be moving back in. Her broker assured her that she was free to do so immediately. So, she did.

19 No I Didn't Adopt ANOTHER Cat! (My Son Did)

The problem is, I have a soft spot for the orphaned kittens. The bottle-fed babies. The hissy, growly, fuzzy, stinky butt bottle baby kittens. When you're manning the office phone for the local humane society, you're the one getting the calls about the orphans that have been discovered in someone's backyard.

Now, let me pause a moment to explain that just because you find kittens and don't see momma, does NOT mean that they are orphaned. Momma cats are known to move kittens from one location to another, and they do this by moving them one at a time. If you come clomping by, momma is going to hide whatever kitten(s) she still has out of sight from you. You may be sitting there watching a couple of kittens, not seeing momma, thinking "Damn, this chick just straight up abandoned her kids!"

And come on. Every mom has thought about doing that at least once in her motherhood. Right? RIGHT? ... No? No. No, God, no. I never thought that when my boys were little and screaming at each other and throwing toys all over the house and dear God is that poop on the walls? No. Motherhood is always rewarding.

Maybe you find a kitten or two without momma in sight. What should you do? Back off. Go back inside. Watch from a window. I mean, certainly make sure they are not in any immediate danger, but don't pick them up and carry them to your local animal rescue and say they were abandoned. Unless momma is dead, they probably weren't. You kidnapped them. And that's felony. I mean, it's a people felony. Not really a kitten felony. But it should be.

I'll also go ahead and use this moment to encourage you to continue monitoring momma and the litter, though, so you can trap them and get them spayed and neutered once the kittens are weaned and old enough. I know. It's complex. And exhausting. But you know what's more exhausting? Figuring out how to deal with the 20 new kittens that show up later that year once these kittens are old enough to breed. It just keeps compounding from there, and those little things start young. We're not talking like a year later. We're talking months. Teen pregnancy is rampant in the cat population.

There is a ton of information about all of this developed by actual educated veterinarian animal expert type people on the interwebs. I'm pretty sure your local vet or animal rescue organization could offer you some excellent advice, as well. Just do a little research if you're truly interested in helping, and you should be. Helping. It's really the best way to live, as one of the helpers, because when people are following Fred Rogers' advice and looking for the helpers, I want them to see me. (And then I want them to get "Won't You Be My Neighbor" stuck in their head and be compelled to hum it for days every time they see me. Because I want to be a helper, but I also want to be a little bit obnoxious so that people develop a very ambiguous response to seeing me. I'm not sure why. I try not to analyze myself too much.)

However, the call I received on this particular day was about a kitten that was weaned, but still quite young. The woman that found him didn't know what to do with him, and she was just visiting from out of town. I agreed to meet her to pick him up. What's one more kitten foster?

But damn. He. Was. Adorable.

A fuzzy little tabby cat with the blue eyes of a kitten. And he was hissy. And spitty. And growly. And he had no idea what to do with toys.

"I don't know who you are, but you can't keep me here forever."

"You want a treat?"

"Of course I want a treat."

"You are the cutest."

"Drop the treat and walk away."

We named him Alexander. We kept him in a crate in the basement initially. We would take turns feeding him and trying to get him to play. We got hisses and growls in return. Finally, Damon suggested that we move Alex's crate to his room so he could work with him more.

So, we did.

And he did.

And gradually Alexander turned into a wildly confident and comical kitten. He and Stinky played well together. Punky had long since given up any hope for me. She judged me constantly, saying my continued need to bring these damn cats into the house was just one more sign to the world that I was a sad, lonely, single woman. I reminded her that she was a cat. She reminded me that she was a princess.

Punky was particularly disgusted by Alexander's habit of lying on his back, legs spread wide to display himself to the world.

"Ick. Put that away. Nobody wants to see that."

I thought perhaps neutering would lead him to be a bit more protective of that area, but no. His pride in his manhood never wavered. He would come sauntering into whatever room you were in, stop in front of whoever happened to draw his attention, and flop dramatically onto his back, legs spread wide, never breaking eye contact. (Even now, years later, he still does this. It's made even more dramatic given his enormous size. Yes, he has grown into a freakishly large cat.)

I listed Alex for adoption for, like, a day, and then my son came to me requesting that we adopt Alex. I didn't really want to adopt him out anyway, so this really was the perfect scenario for me. I could insist that HE adopt Alex (which he did), and I could claim that Alex wasn't technically MY cat (which I do), thus keeping my cat count to what I deemed a reasonable number.

Current editing update:

My son moved out two years ago.

Alex still lives here.

So, there I was, on the floor, talking baby talk to my couch. In fact, I had spent every night on my knees reaching my hand under the couch near where he was hiding and speaking soft, reassuring words to him. Every night. For an entire month. I talked baby talk to my couch.

Then one magical evening it happened. I sat down in my basement, and out of nowhere, this sweet face was looking up at me telling me he was ready now. I had proven myself, and he would now allow me to pet him ... and I did. I sat petting this sweet boy's soft fur for an hour, and then he got up and crawled back under the couch.

It had taken a few months, but today AppleJack (affectionately known in our house as AJ or JackJack) became quite comfortable in his foster home. He still hid when we had visitors, and he had to sleep in the basement because he would torment Punky and Gracie. But he played happily with Alexander and tolerated Lobo. He mostly ignored Pierre.

A few months after he came out of hiding, I thought I might try moving JackJack out into the Cattyshack so I could foster another dog inside without stressing him. I had an entirely new group of cats out there at that point, with the original crew having been adopted into wonderful forever homes. This crew seemed to be pretty chill. They should do well with a new addition.

I coaxed JackJack into a carrier and walked him outside. Once inside the Cattyshack fencing, I opened the carrier and introduced him to the others. There was some hissing, but mostly silence. The first few days, I only took him out to the Shack during the day and brought him back inside at night. I wanted to ease him into it and have easy supervision of what was happening. After several days of no vicious fights, I thought JackJack might be ok to stay overnight.

The morning after his first full night in the Cattyshack, I went out to clean up and feed them all breakfast. JackJack followed me around closely until I left the fencing and began to walk back to the house. I heard someone crying behind me. I turned around and saw JackJack standing up with both front paws clinging to the fencing and crying like my toddler did the first time I left him at a new daycare. It was heartbreaking. Devastating. Unacceptable.

I turned around, packed him back into his crate, and carried him back into the house.

There he would stay until he found that home that would be as patient and tolerant of him as he deserved. A few days later, I was sitting on the couch working, and JackJack climbed up beside me and curled up in my lap. It took him a full six months to get up the courage to do this. It was beautiful.

AppleJack wasn't perfect. He stalked the girl cats. Mind you, he didn't touch them or hiss at them. He would simply walk over to where they were sitting and stare at them...until one of them yelled, hit him, and run away. In a human man, restraining orders would be involved. In my gorgeous AppleJack cat, it was a bit creepy but also rather hilarious.

He smacked my leg and yowled when he felt like he wasn't receiving enough attention...which was every night.

He loved to play fetch with mousey toys, but refused to bring the mousey back so you would have to walk to the other side of the room repeatedly to continue playing.

To watch him run all out, trilling the whole way, and slide across the floor to get to the mousey was pure entertainment. To pet his soft fur and hear the faint purr that he so rarely allows anyone to hear was pure contentment. To look into his eyes and see the gratitude of a being that understands that he has been saved was pure reward.

One morning, JackJack came upstairs immediately angry at the world. The moment I opened the basement door he began hissing and growling at every being that crossed his path. Now, JackJack may not have a perpetually sunny disposition, but this much prissiness was out of the norm for him. However, since I had four other cats demanding food and preparing revolt in exactly one minute and thirteen seconds, I shrugged it off and began the morning feeding routine.

It wasn't until later that morning that I realized what Jack's issue was. It began with Trey saying that someone smelled like poo. Honestly, I figured it was me. It's always me. Why do I always smell like poo? That is an excellent question. It's always me that smells like poo because I am the one assigned to clean up all poo inside and outside the home. I'm the poo lady. Yet, a quick self poo check revealed that the smell was not, in fact, me. I decided to just go about the rest of my morning figuring the source of the poo smell would reveal itself eventually. (Is that weird? Do non-animal rescue people do that? Like, smell poop and make only a casual effort to locate the source then give up figuring you'll find it sooner or later? Because really, don't we have better things to do than to crawl around our house looking for the source of the poop smell?)

Whatever. All you people out there judging, the source DID finally reveal itself. I noticed my handsome JackJack lounging on the coffee table and I snuck in for a quick pet. As I ran my hand down his beautiful, fluffy tail, I located the source of the poo smell. There it was. Poo. Just a big old strand of poo, with a little bit of litter mixed in, just hanging from his tail. Apparently, JackJack had begun to drag the end of his beautiful, fluffy tail through his poo. Well, I can't say for certain that it was his poo he was dragging his tail through, but it's a strong suspicion because, well, why would anyone drag their tail through someone else's poo? I suppose that also begs the question, why would anyone drag their tail through their own poo. Whatever the source of the poo, JackJack had been dragging his tail through it, and it smelled. A lot.

In most of my animals, this would be a simple fix. Just take a washcloth and clean them up. With JackJack, the fix was not so simple. The look in his eye as I approached with a washcloth and began to reach out for his tail made it clear that he wasn't about to let me touch him with a washcloth. He had poo sticking to his tail and it was uncomfortable and embarrassing. He didn't want me anywhere near him. What do you do when you have a poo-caked cat that won't let you touch him?

Well, a braver person may have donned some heavy-duty gloves, scruffed his cute little neck, and forced him into a warm bath. I make no claims of bravery. I grabbed a pair of scissors, belly crawled across the living room floor, and quietly cut the offensive clump of poo fur off of the tip of his tail. Problem solved. Of course, I recognized that this was likely to happen again, and I would eventually need to take a more direct approach before he ended up with a bald tail.

I reminded myself that JackJack and I had established a relationship. We had a history. He loved me. There was no way he would hurt me. Still, I would continue to opt for the scissor belly crawl approach. I mean, Punky loves me, but I still have scars from the last time I tested that love with what she considered inappropriate touching (and by inappropriate touching, I mean that I restrained her while the vet stuck a large needle into the back of her neck).

We hadn't fostered a dog in months, and suddenly this miniature version of my own Lobo was scrolling across my Facebook newsfeed. Except he wasn't like my Lobo. This little one was terrified. Every inch of his body language, from his tucked tail, lowered head, and worried eyes said that life had been hard on him and he knew there was only more bad to come. For a month I wrestled with this photo. Surely someone would fall in love with that sweet, scared little face and adopt him from the pound. I didn't get it. How was he still sitting in the pound all alone?

Then one day my oldest son came home and asked why we hadn't fostered any dogs in a while. Ummmm, because we have a house filled with cats, and I figured one more animal would throw one of us over the edge. A similar conversation with my younger son later that evening made it clear. God wanted me to foster this dog.

The next day, Mindy and I headed to the pound. We walked up and down the rows of kennels talking to all of the sad faces, assuring them we would do what we could to save them. As we neared the last row of kennels, I stopped to videotape a particularly sad face as Mindy moved on to the last row. When I finished, I walked to the end of the row and asked Mindy who was making that god-awful sound.

"Uh, you're foster."

Right. So, THIS was why he wasn't getting any attention in the pound. He was horrifying. I walked to his kennel and heard what he had been screaming to everyone all that time.

"Get the hell away from me! You won't take me alive! Wait! No, I want to stay alive! So, you just don't take me! Don't touch me! Don't you dare touch me! Get away from my kennel! Get away! Don't come in here! I swear if you come in here you're going to lose an arm!"

Yeah, he was a gem. I wondered for a moment if it was too late to change my mind. There was an equally terrified though far less obnoxious little guy in the first row of kennels. I could save him, and he probably wouldn't even try to eat my face. No. No, that wouldn't be right. There was no way this little ball of terror was going to get adopted out of this pound. He had already chased off at least one potential adopter that I knew of. I couldn't back out now and carry his death on my conscience the rest of my life. In that moment I felt like his only chance at life, and I wasn't going to take that away from him. If I lost a limb or two in the process, well at least I hadn't sent him to his death.

The pound staff came back and assured us that he was all bark. I wasn't so sure I believed her, though she had never lied to me before. Still, when she started into the kennel, I cautioned her to be careful. She gave me a condescending smile, walked straight over to Bristol, and picked him up. He promptly peed on her, but he stopped growling. She stood there holding him, and the look in his eyes was sheer terror. We put a leash on him, carried him outside, and sat him on the ground. He immediately folded in on himself, tail tucked and head down as far as it would go. He allowed Mindy to examine him, looking in his mouth and feeling his belly. He made no aggressive moves, no aggressive sounds. He just curled up and waited for a repeat of whatever horrifying things he had experienced before coming to the pound.

Deciding that he would make a great foster with a little work, we signed the transfer paperwork and loaded Bristol into the carrier in my car. I turned on the radio, hoping some music would help him relax.

"What do you like to listen to, Bristol? Country? Hip Hop? Classical?"

Silence.

I went with pop, thinking that, even if it wasn't his favorite, it at least wouldn't depress him or make him angry. We road home somewhat nervously with the sounds of Pink filling the car. I'm not sure either of us took an easy breath during the entire thirty-minute drive. When we pulled into the driveway and I turned off the ignition, there was only silence. I couldn't actually even hear him breathing. I panicked briefly, thinking perhaps he had been so terrified on the ride home that he'd had a heart attack and died. Is that possible? Do dogs have heart attacks? Probably not a dog as young as him, right?

I got out and walked around to the trunk and opened the hatch. I picked up the carrier, placed it on the gravel driveway and knelt down in front of it. The rocks were hard and jagged against my knees, but I was focused on ensuring that this tiny little dog was ok. Opening the carrier door slowly, I cautiously slipped my fingers through the narrow opening to slip the leash over Bristol's tiny little head. He didn't move. He didn't resist or protest. He didn't make a sound. I tugged gently on the leash as I opened the carrier door the entire way.

No response.

I got down on my hands and ducked my head in front of the carrier to get a better view of the terrified Bristol cowering at the back of the carrier.

"It's ok Bristol. You come out now, sweet boy."

Nothing.

"Come on, Bristol," I pleaded. "Won't you please just come out? My knees really hurt and I have treats. You want treats?"

Nope. Still no response. This was going to be a hard case. I had flashbacks to Pearl refusing to let me touch her. Well, it didn't work with her, but maybe it will work with this one. Kneeling there awkwardly on the gravel driveway, tiny pebbles implanting themselves into my hands and larger rocks slicing into my knees, I began to yawn loudly and smack my lips in front of the carrier.

"Ummmmm. Whaaaaat are you doing? What is that? Why are you doing that?" Bristol looked confused, but at least he was responding. "I really think you should stop doing that. It seems a little...odd."

When I realized that the yawning and lip-smacking was only making him more unsettled, I stopped. When I realized that I was quickly losing feeling in my knees, I decided to take a different approach. I stood up unsteadily, still hold onto the leash, and gingerly picked rocks out of my skin.

"Ok, Bristol. If you're not going to come out on your own, I'm gonna help you out."

"What does that mean? What are you --- Whoa!"

Bristol panicked a bit as I slowly tipped the carrier forward, forcing him to slide out the front. He resisted a bit, scrambling his tiny paws on the floor of the carrier. But after a few seconds, he gave up and slid out, where he promptly went into full crouch mode. He was NOT moving.

"Fine. I'm out, but I'm not going anywhere. I don't know you. I don't know what you think you're going to do to me, but I'm staying right here."

I picked him up, and he promptly peed on me.

"Um, that – That was an accident. I didn't mean to do that. I, um, I'm sorry about that," he mumbled.

"It's ok little man. You're ok. You're safe here. Let's go over here in the leaves, and you can go potty before we go inside."

"I don't want – LEAVES!"

As I sat this little, trembling dog down in the leaves, his entire demeanor changed. He began rolling gleefully around and around in the leaves.

"This is AWESOME!"

"Ok, Bristol. I'm glad you like the leaves. Don't you have to go potty?"

He continued to roll around on his back, ignoring me.

I stood there patiently holding onto his leash while he rolled around in utter satisfaction that he was getting the stink of the pound off of him. I promised him a bath as soon as he felt comfortable with me, but he ignored me and just kept rolling. After several minutes, I tugged gently on his leash and asked him to please come inside to see where he would be sleeping. He stood up, shook most of the crushed leaves off of himself, and once again refused to move.

"I'm scared to walk."

"You're scared to- Fine."

I picked him up to carry him into the house and he promptly peed on me again.

"Sorry about that. It's a thing."

"It's ok little guy," I assured him as I carried him into the basement and over to his crate. "See? You've got blankies and toys and your very own food and water. It's nice and quiet. You'll be safe here."

"Uhhhh, ok."

And he crawled cautiously to the back of the crate and curled up in a ball.

No sounds came out of the basement the rest of the night. I went down a few times to check on him. Each time he rolled onto his back, trembling, with his tail tucked up between his legs. He didn't growl or whimper. He also didn't make any moves to welcome me closer. I rubbed his belly each time and whispered reassurances that did nothing to stop his shaking. Eventually I left him be for the night, hoping we could all get some rest.

Upstairs, Stinky and Alex sat anxiously staring at the space between the floor and the basement door.

"Is it another cat?"

"Dog. Definitely smells like a dog."

"It's not even barking."

"I know. It's weird. I don't trust a dog that doesn't bark."

"Do you think she's just gonna keep him down there forever?"

"No. She always keeps them downstairs for a few days so they don't bring any cooties upstairs."

"Oh, yeah. Yeah, you don't want to mess with dog cooties."

It went on like this until Bristol's quarantine was up, and I brought him upstairs to meet the crew.

****

I brought Bristol out of his crate and put his harness and leash on him. When I got up and started walking him toward the basement steps leading upstairs instead of the basement door leading outside, he looked confused.

"Why are we going this way? This isn't where I do the peeing. Why – Wait. Do you mean? You're taking me up there? Up there where all the scary noises are?"

"Scary noises?"

"Yeah! Up there is where the thunder and crashing comes from."

It occurred to me now that it must, indeed, be very loud down here when the boys starting rough-housing and playing with Lobo. I assured Bristol that it was not nearly as scary as it sounded upstairs and gently tugged on his leash. He moved, somewhat reluctantly, up the stairs. I brought him through the open door, and Lobo immediately stuck his nose in Bristol's butt.

"Whoa!" Bristol was clearly overwhelmed by Lobo's intense investigation of his hind parts. "Um, hi. I'm, um, my name is Bristol. What is your name? Could you, uh, hi. Yeah, I'm a boy. Um, lady? Could you ask him to stop?"

"Lobo, stand down, man! Ease up, ok?"

"Oh, yeah, ok. What is it?"

"This is Bristol. He's going to stay with us for a while until he finds his forever home."

"Is he lost?"

"Lobo, seriously. Do we have to go through this with every single foster? He's not lost. He's a foster. He's looking for a new family to live with."

"Oh, yeah. No, I knew that. That's cool. I'm going to go lay down and clean some stuff."

He is such an odd dog, but at least the introduction went well. The cats, however, were not as welcoming. Pumpkin walked past and just sniffed, "I thought we were keeping that downstairs."

"Punky, be nice."

"Whatever. Just stay away from the food, little dog."

Stinky and Alex ran upstairs and hid under the bed and Gracie just continued to nap.

Ok. This was going to be ok. A fairly uneventful introduction is a good thing. Bristol was clearly unfazed by the negativity of the cats. Actually, he barely even seemed to notice them, and that is the way it went for the next few weeks. Bristol and the cats seemed to have some sort of unspoken agreement that neither would acknowledge that the other existed. They seemed quite content with this little arrangement, and it was fine with me if it meant peace in my home.

In general, Lobo did the same until Bristol started acting like an annoying little brother. Lobo would grumble and snap at the little dog. "Back up, small dog! I'm chilling. Go somewhere and calm down."

"Ok. Um, I'll just go chew on this over here."

It was quite clear that Bristol was prepared to submit to whatever rules Lobo put in place. He was just happy to be in an actual home and not sitting in the loud, scary pound waiting to die. He was very clear about how lucky he was and he wasn't about to ruin it by arguing with the big dog that was obviously in charge.

Since the animal population inside my home continues to grow despite my recurring declarations that I cannot take on another foster animal, feeding times have become increasingly complicated. In the past, breakfast and dinner required little more than putting some food in various dishes and ensuring that everyone had access to water. The additions to my animal family over the past year had led to some major complications. One forever dog, one foster dog, four forever cats, one indoor foster cat, and five outdoor foster cats make for hectic mornings. The issue is that it is physically impossible to feed all of them first and each one of them firmly believes he or she should hold feeding priority rights. So, I had to develop a feeding schedule that made the most sense. Here goes. Try to keep up.

Since Stinky has allergies and gets special expensive grain-free food with supplements added, he gets his food first. He gets half a can, so the other half goes back in the fridge until the next day, which is always awesome because I feel compelled to heat that half up a bit in the microwave so it's not too cold for him. This adds precious seconds onto the feeding schedule, so what is stressful one day makes me want to gouge my own eyes out the next.

Anyway, on easy days I wake to Punky and Stinky arguing over which one is going to wake me up while Alexander sits at my head staring at me and Lobo lays at my feet cleaning himself. I always lie there for several minutes refusing to believe it's time to get up. The more complicated the feeding schedule becomes, the more reluctant I am to get out of bed. The hissing, growling, and staring becomes increasingly insistent until I finally sit up and drag myself out of the bed, down the stairs, and to the special closet that contains all of the food and finally pull out two cans of food.

This is where it gets complicated, and sometimes even a little ugly. I open Stinky's food first and try to pacify Punky and hold Stinky back while I mix his food and supplements up on a saucer. At my feet, Alexander yells loudly and Bristol jumps around excitedly until Punky hisses and smacks at him. Lobo sits to the side quietly waiting his turn, while Gracie and AppleJack try to remain out of sight until it's their turn to eat.

"Momma! The food, momma! I need the food!" Stinky and Alexander yell in unison.

"Lady, can't you move any faster? I'm dyyyyyyying." Punky can be a little dramatic.

By the time I'm done mixing Stinky's food, he dives right in and Punky has worked herself into a tizzy. Despite the fact that I have fed her every morning for two solid years, she seems to be under the delusion that today is the day that I will skip her, and she will immediately fall over dead from starvation.

"Honestly, I swear you get slower every day. You are the slowest person in the world." Punky is not a groveler. Really, she just takes to insulting the hand that feeds her. Meanwhile, Bristol is having a near-panic attack at my side.

"Pet meeeeeee! I need to be petted! Pleeeeease, foster momma lady. I neeeed to be petted!" He had turned into a clingy little thing.

I continue on to the next can of food and divide it between the remaining four cats, though not evenly. Punky gets a full half of the can and she's mumbling under her breath until I finally put the saucer in front of her. Alexander continues yelling until he gets his saucer with one quarter of the can. This leaves one more quarter of a can to split between Gracie and AppleJack. I split it between the two of them and they cautiously approach the saucers of scrapings leftover from the bottom of the can.

"Are you sure Punky got enough?" Gracie asks quietly before taking a timid bite.

"Yeah, I don't need her drama this early in the morning before I've had my coffee."

"You don't drink coffee, Jack Jack."

"Oh yeah. Well, then I REALLY don't need her drama this early."

No sooner do Gracie and Jack begin to take a few bites of their food than Punky and Alexander finish theirs and set out in seek of other food sources. Punky barrels across the room to Gracie's saucer and without saying a word, pushes Gracie out of the way and begins eating her food. Jack Jack, not wanting to take any chances, quickly surrenders his saucer without even being challenged. He disappears back to the basement. Gracie disappears to some other unknown spot. Meanwhile, Alexander has moved over to Stinky's saucer and is forcing his head between the food and Stinky's mouth, inhaling whatever food is still left.

Amidst this chaos, Bristol continues to jump up on me while I pull Lobo's morning treat out of the treat cabinet and hand it to him. Lobo takes it eagerly and offers a quick, "Thanks, mom" before hurrying into Damon's room to get to work chewing through the rawhide. With the standard crew finally cared for, I pick up Bristol's leash and walk him to the door.

"Outside? Are we really going outside? I love outside? Are you coming outside, too? Let's go outside together!"

"Come on, Bristol. It's time to go potty."

We wander around the back yard for a few minutes until Bristol finds a suitable spot for the pottying. The Cattyshack Crew watch eagerly, asking when the little dog will be finished so they can have their breakfast.

"Yeah, um, we don't wanna rush his, um, special morning habit time. But, um, well, Chrissy ate all the food from last night, and the rest of us are kind of hungry." Albert was always such a sweetheart. But Bristol always seemed unfazed by the group of cats gathered to watch him impatiently as he did his business.

"I did not eat ALL of the food, Albie. Jack had some, too. But, yeah, we're starving. Could you hurry it up, little dog?"

We enter the Cattyshack to a swarm of hungry felines, each shouting up at me about the poor service and lack of qualified employees. Bristol busies himself with a cat toy while I divide a can of food among the five cats. Again, there is a specific feeding order that must be followed. Chrissy sits at the top of the food hierarchy, as is evidenced by her round belly. Tiny little Janet has managed to position herself right behind Chrissy in the hierarchy. I suspect she plays on the sympathies and chivalry of the boys, insisting that she is such a small little girl that she must eat before them. Albie and Jack seemed to buy it, as they always waits patiently for the girls to get their food first. Andy, however, wasn't buying into the helpless waif image so he hovered eagerly over Janet as she receives her helping. The only thing keeping him from diving into her food was a tiny sliver of chivalry that demanded he allow the girl to go first, but just barely.

Bristol was a challenging one to find the right home for. I think a foster parent's biggest fear is that one of their former fosters ending up back at the pound. We also fear that call that tells us a foster is coming back because when we place a foster into a forever home, there is a relief that comes along with the sadness. Many of us have our own pets, and we accommodate more animals than we truly have the time and space for so that we can save lives. So, when we send a foster onto a forever home, we are able to breathe again for a moment. The workload decreases just a bit, and we can fall back into normal schedules. Our homes relax a bit more. Our family members fall back into sync.

Still, there are those fosters that, when we do get that call, we are not fully surprised. We often take chances on the less adoptable ones, and we know that not every adoption will be perfect. We try to avoid bad situations by carefully screening potential adopters and ensuring that the home environment is the right one for that animal's temperament. Unfortunately, even with all of the discussion and worry and laboring over the decision, things still go wrong.

Bristol was a fearful dog. I'm not sure he will ever be fully secure in any environment. Yet, during his time with me, he was never aggressive and seemed easily comforted when new people visited. He was generally calm and quiet and just easy-going. But in his new home, he was a different animal. He decided that it was up to him to be the protector of the family. He chased down anyone who dared visit, growling and baring his teeth. He yowled and whined incessantly when crated at night. He bullied and injured their other slightly smaller dog. He even showed aggression towards children, and that is something you just can't take a chance on.

It broke his adoptive family's heart, because they truly were in love with him. They were devastated to have to give up on him, but sometimes these things are blessings in disguise. When he came back, we tried him out at a new foster home. It was a foster home with several other dogs already, and I suspect having a larger pack allowed him to be kept in line more easily. He did well there, and his foster family quickly fell in love with him and became his new forever family.

They don't always have an easy path to get where they're going. We just have to keep them safe and try to stay patient while they find their way through us.

"What exactly are you chewin on over there, Punky?"

"Nothin," she mumbled.

"Looks like you're chewing on an electrical plug that happens to be plugged in."

"Mmmm?" She continued gnawing.

"Do you know why they call them electrical plugs?"

Gnaw, gnaw, gnaw.

"Because when you plug them in, like the one you have in your mouth right now, electricity comes out."

Gnaw, gnaw, gnaw.

Why? Why do cats do weird things? She was obviously pouting about something, and this was her way of letting me know. But why this? Why one of the single-most dangerous behaviors that could not only kill her, but leave us all homeless? Fine.

"So, um, something you wanna talk about, Punk?" She paused for a moment and glared at me. "I, um. Should I already know what you want to talk about?"

"Really?" she sighed. "Fine. You took that fatty Alexander to terrifying office of doom last week."

"You mean the vet's office? I took him to the vet's office?"

"You say vet's office. I say terrifying office of doom. Whatever. I KNOW they told you to stop feeding him so much because I heard him and the smelly one talking about it."

"Well, she said that could be one of the issues, but she also said he probably needs to exercise more."

"No. No, he exercises enough when he chases me around the house every night. And I don't run because I'm afraid of him. I just run because I'm worried he'll fall on top of me and crush me with his fat butt."

"Punky, he's not really fat. He's just built a little bigger than you."

"He's fat. He's fat and he has a tiny little head and stubby little legs and he needs to stop eating so much. You're still giving him the same amount of food in the morning's when the rest of us who AREN'T fat could be getting a little extra!"

"You know, Punk, Alex gets the smallest helping out of all of you. You're already getting almost twice what the other cats are getting."

"Exactly. 'Almost.' He's fat and he needs less food. I'm slim, and I need more food. If I had thumbs I'd take over the food distribution myself and save you the trouble. But I don't. So I need you to figure this out and get a little better at it. So. Take whatever you are currently feeding the fat one, cut it in half, and give the bigger half to me."

"Punky, that seems a little extreme. He's already getting less than half of what you get. The poor boy has to eat something."

"Look, whatever. Then just give me half of the smelly one's share. I don't care. I'm tired of arguing with you. Just do what you have to do to get me more food. Make it happen!" And at that, she got up and walked away. Attitude. Pure attitude.

The next morning, I walked to the food pantry and pulled out the cans of food for the cats and walked to the feeding table. Punky sat there smugly, smirking a bit at Alex and Stinky, quite certain that the food allotments were going to reflect her insistence on more food. I opened Stinky's can of food and gave him his designated half. I then opened the second can and gave Punky her half. She immediately began devouring the food on her plate and then noticed that I was spooning a full quarter of the can onto Alexander's plate before carrying the rest over to Gracie's eating spot under the feeding table.

She didn't actually stop eating in order to draw my attention to my complete failure to follow her instructions. "Ahem. This is not what we agreed on," she mumbled through a mouthful of food.

"You're fine, Punky. Just eat your breakfast and let everyone else eat theirs in peace."

"This is not-" she began before choking on the food she had half-swallowed. "Hack. Hack." She began trying to cough the food back up so she could start over. It's really difficult to look indignant and superior when you're hacking up food.

"Perhaps you should focus on eating your food without hurting yourself and let everyone else worry about themselves."

HACK! At that, she rolled her eyes at me and turned back to her food. She mumbled something I couldn't quite make out, which is probably best. I had other animals to feed, anyway.

25 HOW I LEARNED MY PETS ARE A-HOLES

Another miniature Lobo. How do I keep ending up with these small, adorable dogs that look just like my baby boy? They tear at my heart. This little girl came from a hoarding situation, so she was damaged. She had actually spent months with another foster family learning how to trust. She was described as being one of those dogs you can't go near. They had to feed her through the fencing. She was completely unsocialized. Over the months, however, her foster family managed to get close enough to her to pet her and feed her without fear of being attacked. Still, when they said they needed to move all of their fosters out, I reluctantly agreed to take on what I thought was their most difficult case.

When I showed up at the adoption event where they were bringing her for me to pick up, I anticipated a growly, bristly dog. What I found was a trembling, cowering little girl trying her best to make herself invisible at the back of her crate. However, I've been down this road before. I've seen those trembling, cowering dogs turn vicious in a heartbeat. I cautiously loaded her into a carrier, placed her in my car, and drove her home.

It was several minutes, after arriving home, before I could get her out of the carrier. I had to make sure Lobo and the cats were safely upstairs and carry in all of my supplies. Finally, when I opened the carrier to let her out, I saw that she was covered in vomit. Literally, head to tail, covered in puke.

"I get car sick," she said in a small voice. "I'm sorry."

She tucked her little tail and stared down at the ground as I coaxed her out of the carrier and up the porch steps to the gated deck. She had no idea what was coming and it probably wasn't the best plan for a fearful dog in a brand new environment, but she had to have a bath.

"NOOOOOOO! PLEASE STOP!" I didn't expect such a small dog to have so much fight in her, but she did everything short of biting me in an attempt to escape. The look in her eyes told me she was terrified, and she was strongly considering taking a nice chunk out of my hand. To her credit, she did not. She simply wriggled and whined and pleaded to me to stop spraying water all over her. Within ten minutes, I had managed to wash off the filth and rinse out the shampoo and let go of her collar. She ran to the opposite end of the deck and cuddled in the corner by the door.

"That wasn't very nice."

Still, she allowed me to towel her off a bit and carry her down to the basement where her crate was waiting with cozy blankets, water, and food. She crawled to the back of the crate and sat trembling, saying nothing.

"You just relax here for a while. Eat some dinner and take a nap. You've had a long day." Silence. She was decidedly not speaking to me.

I visited her several times that night just to see how she was doing. Each time I looked into her crate she would start trembling and cower further to the back. She still wasn't speaking to me and didn't care to even look at me. Eventually I left her alone for the night, hoping that she would get some rest and wake up in the morning with more willingness to interact.

The next morning, I thought I'd try to take her for a nice, long walk to help her acclimate. I've always found that even the most terrified of dogs almost immediately relax on a walk. I went downstairs carrying her leash, and when I approached her crate I saw the slightest wag of her tail. Then she apparently remembered she was still not speaking to me, and she returned to her cowering. When it became clear that she was not going to come out on her own even after I opened the door and showed her the leash, I decided to crawl in and get her.

She didn't fight me. She didn't growl or whine. She just allowed me to attach her leash, clumsily pull her out of the crate, and carry her outside. Once outside, she immediately relaxed. Her tail went up and her nose went to the ground.

"Oh, this is fun!"

We walked the mile to my parents' house with Derby insisting on following me rather than walking next to me. If I stopped and turned around, she would immediately sit and look up at me expectantly with head slightly braced as though she anticipated being struck. Each time I would reassure her and encourage her to walk beside me.

"No, thank you. I am fine back here. I can still smell the smells this way."

We arrived at my parents' house, and Derby's eyes lit up when she saw my mom's large ceramic cat sitting on the porch.

"A cat! I LOVE cats! That's the biggest cat I've ever seen! Hi, cat! Wait…This cat isn't real!" She looked up at me somewhat confused. "Why would someone put a fake cat on their porch when they could just get a real one? The real ones are much more fun."

At that point she realized that my parents had come out to meet her, and she quickly backed down off the porch as much as the leash would allow. My mom tried to coax her with treats, but she wasn't taking the bait. As I sat on the porch trying to ease her concern and convince her that everything was ok, something magical happened. Derby walked up the porch steps and into my lap. It was only for a moment. She gave me a quick kiss on the chin and then moved back a few steps to lie down.

It is always amazing to me when this happens. To experience the moment when trust is established with such a broken soul is, indeed, magical.

Over the next few weeks, Derby became increasingly comfortable in my house. She slept in her crate in the basement at night and under my desk at my feet during the day. Every morning after feeding all of the indoor animals, I would go downstairs and get Derby. We would go outside so she could go potty and then she would run full out to the Cattyshack, eager to greet her new friends. The Crew would yell good morning to her and reach through the fencing to give her a pat on the nose until I got there to let her in.

While I cleaned out the litter boxes and refilled the water, Derby took time greeting each cat and even to groom Andy, Albert, and Jack. Chrissy and Janet, while excited to see Derby, were not about to let a dog give them a bath. They said it would be like bathing in a mud puddle. The boys seemed oblivious to the girls' complaints, though. They were happy to get a quick morning bath.

While I put out the breakfast, the Crew quickly forgot Derby was there and clamored for food. Derby then took time to sniff around the floor cleaning up any dropped pieces or finding a mousey toy to chew on. Once I finished my Cattyshack chores, Derby and I would go back in the house so I could get to work. She would curl up under my desk at my feet and lie there quietly until it was time for our afternoon potty break. At that she would jump up, and the excitement of the day would reenergize her.

We quickly fell into this easy routine, and it worked well for the first week. It wasn't long, though, before Lobo began acting out. He started yelling at Derby for the littlest thing. In truth, I usually had no idea why he was yelling at her. Still, the small dog refused to submit to the big dog, and she would go right back at him. Within days I was breaking up daily fights. Much like the at-risk youth I'd worked with in the past, these two seemed to be mostly bark. They would bare teeth, snarl, growl, and appear to be involved in a vicious fight. But in reality, it was mostly a lot of threats and fake punches being thrown. Both always walked away without a mark on them, and they always made sure I was around to break up the fight before any real damage could be done.

However, things took a more serious turn for Derby when Alexander got in on Lobo's bullying. Clearly trying to impress his favorite brother, Alex would follow Derby around in a cat-stalking pose and stare at her tauntingly. Derby refused to make eye contact, and the first time Alex actually hit her, she screamed and ran for the other side of the house desperately looking for a safe place to hide. Sadly, there are no safe places to hide from a cat. They can get anywhere she can, so she was at his mercy until I intervened.

One day I went upstairs to get a book and Derby followed me up. I didn't really think much of it when she didn't follow me back down to the living room. I actually thought she had gone on down to the basement to hang out with my son or relax in her crate. It wasn't until an hour later that I noticed she still wasn't cuddled close by like she normally does. Then I heard a faint whimper from upstairs. I looked up at the loft and saw Gracie staring down at me. When I looked at her questioningly, she just rolled her eyes and went back to sleep. She had no interest in helping out small dog or getting involved in the drama that was unfolding upstairs.

So I walked over to the stairs to see if Derby was afraid to come down for some reason. I mean, she is a small dog with small legs, so maybe she felt like she couldn't maneuver the steps. What I found, however, was a very smug looking Alexander sitting calmly at the top of the stairs. He looked at me blankly for a moment, then went back to staring at something just out of my line of sight.

"Alex, do you have Derby up there?" At the sound my voice, Derby came scrambling around the corner and stepped down on the top step. Alex refused to give way and sat staring at her threateningly.

"Alexander! Stop being such an asshole!" At that, Derby quickly began scrambling down the rest of the steps, eventually losing her footing and sliding down the rest of the way and slamming head first into the wall. She quickly jumped up and continued slipping and running to get to the couch. At the sight of Derby losing her footing and sliding uncontrollably down the stairs, Alex began rolling around and laughing hysterically.

"Did you see that, Lobo! It was hilarious!"

Lobo was too busy cleaning himself to notice. Pumpkin snickered a few times, then went back to sleep. Stinky popped his little head up off the couch to see what the ruckus was and asked, "You ok, mama?" Gracie never even stirred.

Not a single animal in my home exhibited even the slightest concern for the small dog. They were uncaring, ungrateful, spoiled little brats that had clearly forgotten that every single one of them had also been a foster at some point.

"But I love cats. I don't understand why he is so mean to me. Doesn't he know I love cats?" Yeah, this little girl needed a new home free of bullies and she needed one quickly.

****

"Where are we going?" Derby looked at the carrier curiously and then quickly began trembling.

"We're not going back to the bad place, are we? I promise I won't fight with Lobo anymore. He can tell me what to do. I promise!"

"It's fine, baby girl. We're gonna go meet your new mama today."

"Ok, but then we get to come back home, right?"

We drove mostly in silence. I heard an occasional worried mumble from the back of the car.

"What does she mean 'new mama?' Hey! What do you mean 'new mama?!'"

Silence.

"She brought my medicine. Why did she bring my medicine yummy treats if we're only going to say hi to someone? I mean, we're coming back."

116

Another short silence.

"Hey! Why did you bring my medicine yummy treats if we're coming back?!"

More silence.

"I don't know. This seems wrong."

Eventually I just turned the music up. Listening to her worry was more than I could handle. She'd only been with me for a few weeks, but she had already made her way into my heart. The broken ones always do that.

It has gotten easier to let them go, but when they get all worried and quiet, it really becomes quite difficult. Once we got to the event where her new adoptive mom would meet her, I brought her out of the carrier and she calmed down a bit.

"Oh, this looks fun! There are a lot of people, but smell all of the smells! Are those sausage biscuits? Can we get some?"

Derby spent the morning wagging her tail and following me closely. She allowed some visitors to pet her and others she shied away from. When her new mama arrived, we moved away from the crowd and sat on the grass in the sunshine. Derby sat in between us, looking up at me questioningly.

"This is your new mama. She wants you to go live with her. And guess what. She has cats. Two of them. And they love dogs."

Derby looked up at her new mama. "Really?"

She allowed her new mama to pet her, nudging her hand to keep going if it looked like she might stop. I didn't expect her to immediately climb into her new mama's lap or follow her eagerly around. It doesn't usually work that way. But the mere fact that she was seeking out more pets was a comforting sign. She was not cowering away from her or trembling too much.

When it was clear that this was going to work, Derby's new mama asked if I could follow her to the store where she could buy a carrier to take Derby home in. We drove a few miles up the road and Derby was silent the whole way. She was clearly a bit unsettled and confused, though she didn't appear to be frightened. As we waited for her mama to go in to buy a carrier, Derby and I shared some last peaceful moments sitting in a small grassy area of the parking lot.

"I'm really going to miss you, small dog. You are such a sweet, sweet girl, and you're going to be so happy in your new home. Your mama is going to love you and cuddle you and keep you safe always. You are such a brave girl, and I am so proud of you."

Derby sat there with her front paws on my lap staring silently up at me. She didn't say a word. She didn't cry or tremble. She seemed to understand and accept that her time with me was only temporary and that her amazing new life was about to begin.

As I loaded her into her mama's car, I handed her one of the towels she had kept in her crate at my house. I didn't cry. I said goodbye to her and told her I loved her. I didn't cry. I hugged her new mama and thanked her for giving this special little girl the safe and loving forever home that she deserved. I didn't cry. Then she closed the back door and got in her car. I turned and got into mine, immediately starting up the car and driving away. I didn't cry. The tears were there. They lingered at the backs of my eyes, but they didn't come out. This was a happy moment, and I refused to ruin it with tears.

I drove home contemplating the break we were going to take from dog fostering. Lobo clearly needed it. He was just getting increasing temperamental as he aged, and he needed a break from the parade of new dogs coming through his home. I would still have the Cattyshack. They were outside and caused no concern for any of my indoor animals. In fact, Alexander seemed to enjoy going out on the balcony and yelling down at the Crew on days when I would keep the door open.

Still, it would be odd to have so much peace in the house for an extended time. Well, it would be as peaceful as a house can be with two teenaged boys, four cats, and a large dog, but this is what

Lobo clearly needed. He was tired of fostering and wanted his house to himself for a while. He was tired of giving back. He wanted to be an only dog again. That was fair enough.

When I arrived home and walked into the house, Lobo greeted me eagerly and then had the nerve to look up at me and ask, "Where is the small dog?" as though he hadn't just spent the past two weeks tormenting her daily and hoping for her to move out.

Winter hits, and it is unusually cold here in Virginia. Even with a space heater, I can't keep the Cattyshack warm enough to allow me to sleep soundly at night. I worry about the crew out there shivering and huddled together. They're cats, of course, so they were fine. They had adequate shelter, heat, and lots of cuddly blankets. I knew this, but still I couldn't rest with them outside and the rest of us comfortably inside a relatively warm house. It was only relatively warm because the open multistory floor plan requires two heat pumps to adequately heat and cool, but at some point one of those heat pumps gave out. I simply couldn't afford to get it fixed, so we made due with one sad little heat pump that barely managed to keep the house at 64 degrees on a truly cold day. Still, 64 degrees was practically a sauna compared to the 8 degrees outside, and my Cattyshack Crew deserved to enjoy it, too.

I didn't consult the indoor residents. I briefly mentioned it to my sons who use the basement as a man cave when their friends visit, but the decision was made. The Cattyshack Crew moved into the basement. Five of them. In the basement. That brought the total number of felines in the home to nine. Now, I recognize that "a lot" is a subjective term, but nine cats inside a modest single-family home is a lot. A LOT.

Pumpkin was the first to question me.

"The others asked me to talk to you. You know I wouldn't complain, but the others, you know. They're concerned. They want me to talk to you about this whole fostering thing. Well, and about your image. You're getting older now. You'll be forty this year and, well, you're still single. It just doesn't look good to have this many cats, a woman of your age and lack of dating prospects. So, you know, because we love you – and this is totally about you – we think it's best that you stop with the cats. And dogs, too. And probably kids. So, really, just no new residents. And, well, it might be a good idea to start scaling back, you know? The ones in the basement should probably just go back outside. No reason for that lovely shack to sit empty all winter. They'll be fine. And it might not be a bad idea to put a few from up here onto some sort of adoption site. You have access to those, right? Maybe the slobbery one and the smelly one, to start. The chubby one could probably go, too. I think you'd be surprised at how much cleaner and easier your life would be with just me to care for. Oh, yeah, the quiet one should go, too. She worries me."

"Well, Punk, that was a nice little speech and I truly appreciate your obviously sincere concern for my well-being. It's unnecessary, I assure you. I have no desire to date, and I really don't mind cleaning up behind you guys. It's fine, really."

"Fine. You want to make this hard, we can do that. Either the basement cats GO or things might start to get a little ugly around here."

"What do you mean by ugly, Punky? Are you threatening me?"

"YES! I'm going to start breaking random things and telling the chubby one to pee in places that are not a litterbox."

"Punky, you are too cute when you're pissy. It'll all be fine, momma. Why don't you just go take a little nap." With that, I patted her calico head and walked away. Later, I heard her by the basement door grumbling what I assume were little threats to the Cattyshack cats that were lingering at the top of the basement steps hoping for a glimpse at the world upstairs. I'm pretty sure I could make out the words "traumatic" and "loss of life." Eventually, Stinky and Alex joined her in an odd showing of unity among the upstairs residents. It was unsettling.

Still, the Cattyshack Crew remained unfazed by Punky's threats. Every time I would open the door to go down for feeding time, Albert and Janet eagerly poked their head through admiring the plush couch and table full of food. They were oblivious to the cold stares and grumbles coming from Punky and her gang, and make no mistake, they were a gang. I have no idea what sort of initiation she forced Alex and Stinky to endure, but they were clearly her rather unimpressive muscle.

After a few weeks, I decided to let Lobo come downstairs with me so I could see how the Crew did with him. I knew they loved watching him play outside from behind the secure fencing of the Cattyshack, but I was curious how they would handle 90 lbs. of slobbery fur hovering over them and smelling on them.

When we first got downstairs, there was not a cat to be seen. But as soon as they heard the tip tap of Lobo's paws on the floor, cats emerged from under every couch and chair in the room. They swarmed him excitedly, purring and rubbing up against him, vying for his attention.

"DOG!!! We missed you, dog!"

"Where were you guys?" I asked.

"We were in the sleeping spots," Albert explained, as though I were an idiot.

"What sleeping spots? Under the couches?"

"Well, yeah. They're all stuffed with the comfy fluffy. Why? How do YOU sleep in them?"

I sighed. They had found AppleJack's holes. Five cats crawling around inside the couches couldn't be good for the integrity of the couches, but what could I do?

For the next thirty minutes, the cats took turns flopping down in front of Lobo, and Lobo smelled and cleaned each one. I should say he attempted to clean each one, though the slobber he left behind left them looking anything but clean. When it was Jack's turn, he dutifully flopped down in front of Lobo, and Lobo responded by wrapping his mouth around Jack's entire head.

"Look, Al!" Jack shouted excitedly. "I can fit my whole head inside of his mouth!"

With that, the two began romping and playing. Lobo pounced and Jack rolled. Jack leapt, and Lobo crouched, preparing to pounce again. It was the oddest sight I'd seen, a 90 pound dog romping and playing with a ten pound cat. The two tired within minutes, and by the time they walked away, Jack looked like he had just stepped out of the shower.

I took Lobo downstairs to visit with the Cattyshack Crew regularly over the next few weeks, until I began allowing the Crew upstairs in pairs to see how they adjusted to a regular household environment with new cats. Janet and Albert were the first to come up. Pumpkin was disgusted.

"I thought we kept those things downstairs."

"They just want to come up and enjoy the family, Punk."

"What's wrong with her?" Pumpkin asked me one day.

"What do you mean? There's nothing wrong with her."

"There's SOMETHING wrong with her. Have you seen her? She just walks around talking to everything. Yesterday I saw her talking to a wall."

"Don't be so pissy, Punk. Janet's just friendly."

"She's special."

"Yes, she is."

"I didn't mean a good kind of special. I mean the kind of special where she lulls you into a sense of peace and then she kills you in your sleep."

"Punk, YOU are that kind of special."

"Nah. With me you know it's coming. I just haven't figured out how to grip a knife yet." She paused for a moment. "I would like you to make her go away now."

"Pumpkin, you know she'll get adopted when she gets adopted. Just try to be pleasant."

"Make her go away now."

"If you can't be pleasant then just ignore her."

"I do ignore her. Always. She talks to me anyway. I don't like it. Make her go away now, please."

"Punk."

"I said please. I don't say please. Ever. Make her go away. Now. Please."

It was true, though. Janet was just happy and she talked to everyone. And everything. She would walk up and just ask you how you were doing. What you had for breakfast. If you had any plans for the weekend. And she asked everyone, including Pumpkin, who would inevitably respond with some sort of profanity. Janet would stand and stare at her for a moment, I suppose processing how someone who had such an easy life could be so unhappy. Then she would shrug and move on to the next person. Or cat. Or dog. Or chair. Or lamp.

Coincidentally, shortly after my conversation with Punky, we decided to start moving the Cattyshack Crew on to areas where they would get more exposure. I mean, I wasn't exactly afraid of Punky, but she seemed to have formed an odd alliance with Stinky and Alex and that just seemed like a very unstable situation.

The first to go was Janet. She went to a local animal emergency clinic where we would send cats to get more exposure by potential adopters. Janet met hers within a day. It was not surprising, with her sweet, chatty nature. I wasn't there when it happened, but I imagine it going something like this.

"Hi there, lady. I'm sorry about your dog. My name is Janet. I like dogs. And treats. And conversation. Wanna hang out?" And the lady did. And so now Janet is undoubtedly providing endless conversation and entertainment to the sweet lady who had just lost her best friend and needed someone to help ease the pain and loneliness. Who better than this special little girl?

The next to go was Jack. However, I was concerned about Jack's ability to adjust to a new setting, as Lobo was the only one who could make him emerge from inside the couch at my house. So, we decided he would go back to HQ and move back in with his sister, Allie, in the colony room. I was somewhat worried about his ability to even adjust back to that environment, but he did fine. He was the handsome new strapping young man in a room filled with ladies...and McDreamy. McDreamy, handsome in his own right, was decidedly not strapping, and prior to Jack's arrival, he'd been the man of the house. You can see where he might not welcome Jack with open arms, but Jack, much like his sister, was oblivious to the negativity.

Shortly after Jack's move, Albert took his sister's place at the animal emergency clinic. He was far less comfortable than Janet being in this new environment. He apparently spent much of his time hiding in plants. The staff took this as a sign of his maladjustment, but I suspect he was just doing his best Johnny English impression.

This left Chrissy and Andy in the basement. Within days of being the last two remaining, they were at the top of the steps begging to come upstairs. Every trip downstairs to feed them was a test of my proprioception. (You like that word? Proprioception. I learned that one as a trail runner. Trail runners need good proprioception to avoid falling off the side of a mountain.)

"Please can we just be upstairs? We'll be good. We promise!" Their sweet little faces begged, and I just couldn't say no. So, every morning after breakfast (because I was not about to combine feeding times), I would let them come upstairs. Things worked well for the first few days, but at some point, both Chrissy and Andy caught on to the fact that Pumpkin did not like to be looked at. I'm not sure why it took them so long to catch onto that because everyone in the house knows it's a rule that we don't look at Pumpkin. We definitely don't make eye contact with Pumpkin, so, why it took them so many days to learn this, I'm not sure. Once they caught on, pure chaos ensued.

They would take turns. At first it was just Chrissy. She would just sit and stare at Pumpkin from across the room. Then she would get up and move a little closer, all the while just staring. It was not a threatening stare, mind you. In fact, she seemed almost peaceful in her staring, as though she were trying to will Pumpkin to be pleasant. I quickly learned, however, that there was nothing peaceful in her staring because when Pumpkin would get up, curse, and walk to another part of the house, Chrissy would follow her. Staring. Pumpkin would run. Chrissy would run. Staring. Pumpkin would call her a demon cat and throw something at her (always something of mine and always something breakable, of course), and Chrissy would duck then stare. When they felt that Pumpkin was not reacting strongly enough, Andy would join in. So, it would be the two of them. Staring. At Pumpkin. I actually began to feel bad for her.

Turns out I wasn't the only one. One weekend, my son had some friends over for the Super Bowl. They stayed for two days, a basement filled with teenage boys. Since I had ended upstairs time for the Cattyshack Crew, Chrissy and Andy were stuck in the basement with the boys. Chaos. That is what a single room filled with teenaged football and soccer players for two whole days is. Chaos. Chrissy seemed to handle it well, just hanging out with the guys and playing Playstation. Andy, however, struggled.

Just before midnight Saturday, as I was trying to ignore the sounds of madness drifting up from the basement, I began to hear crying.

"Hello? Hello? Foster lady Sunshine? Hello? Can I come upstairs? PLEEEEEEASE?"

It was Andy, I could tell.

"Hello?"

He sounded so sad. So pathetic. So frightened. The next morning my son and his friends would explain that Andy had been doing that for two hours by the time I heard him. Each time he started crying, one of them would go up to open the door for him, and he would retreat back down the stairs in one giant leap. They thought they heard him yell something like "You'll never take me alive, humans!" as he went.

When I heard his sad little pleas, though, I couldn't handle it. I crawled begrudgingly out of bed and stumbled down to the basement door. I opened it to see Andy staring up at me with wide, innocent eyes. "Please?"

"Ok, you can come upstairs. But it's night night time so you must find a spot and go to sleep. Whatever you do, you must not look at Punky. In fact, she's upstairs. You stay in the living room. Got it?"

"Got it. I promise."

I stepped aside to let him up and he gave me a gleeful little purr as he rubbed past my legs. Then I walked back upstairs and crawled into bed. Still warm. Happy. I quickly began to drift off to sleep. Just before I floated back into a peaceful little dream, I heard it.

"WHAT THE HELL ARE YOU STARING AT?????"

Oh goodness. No no no no no no NO!

"Andrew!"

"What?"

"I told you to stay away from Pumpkin!"

"I did stay away from Pumpkin!" Andy was vehemently protesting as I walked into my office area to find him sitting directly in front of an explosive Punky. In that moment, I was less angry with Andy for waking me and more concerned for the safety of every single being in the house, and where was Lobo? He was always my backup, ready to yell aggressively at any cat whose name I said in an annoyed voice. Nowhere. He was nowhere to be found. Coward.

In an attempt to at least convince Pumpkin that I was not to blame for interrupting her sleep, I quickly said, "Andrew. I told you, leave Pumpkin alone. Downstairs. Now!"

Pumpkin stared coldly at me for a moment, continuing the low, guttural growl that she had been doing since I came into the room. In fact, I don't remember her ever stopping. Didn't she have to breathe at some point?

"Fine. But I did leave her alone. I mean, for, like, two whole minutes I didn't even look at her." He grumbled the entire way back to the basement. "I don't know why it's such a big deal. She's so sensitive. She's mentally unstable, you know. You should look into medicating her. I bet Xanax would take care of it. You know, there's a pretty high incidence of mental illness in the offender population."

"You heard me say that during one of my class lectures."

"Well, it's true, right? You should probably be careful. She's not stable."

"I know she's not stable, Andrew. That's why I told you to leave her alone. We don't look at Punky. Ever. It's a rule."

"Seems like it would just be easier to send her to live someplace else. You know, I hear they take good care of the cats over at the pound."

I opened the door. "Good night, Andrew. Nobody's going to the pound."

"You call me Andrew when you're mad at me, right?"

"I call you Andrew when I'm tired, and you refuse to follow the rules."

"Oh. Ok. Well, maybe you should tell these kids down here to be quiet so you can sleep."

"Good night, Andrew."

"Yeah. Ok. Night." And he slunk back down the stairs, glancing back every so often to see if I would change my mind.

I didn't.

The next morning, my son and his friends would describe the events after I sent Andy back to the basement.

"That black and white one is evil," my son proclaimed over breakfast.

"What do you mean, evil? My Andy is a sweetheart. He's my favorite."

"He's evil and he wants to hurt me."

"Stop it."

"It's true. He stands behind a wall and peaks one eye around the edge just staring at me. As soon as I look at him, he jumps back behind the wall. I look away and he starts staring again."

"You're worse than Pumpkin. He's just looking at you. Ignore him."

"Then when I fell asleep, he started creeping towards me like Chucky."

His friends started chiming in at this point. "I'm pretty sure he had a shiv. You should never have let him out of AlCATraz. He spent all his time on the rec yard lifting weights."

"Yeah, he's all tatted up under that fur, you know."

"I think I smelled him making mash last night, too."

"How do you guys even know what mash is?"

27 A Place With A Couch?

"Person! New person! Hi new person lady!" Bella greeted me eagerly when I entered Pat's house. She was a sweet little Fox Terrier mix. She jumped up gently to greet me. I had seen her pictures on Facebook, but this was my first time meeting her. She needed to get her vaccinations updated before going to a local kennel for boarding until we could find a foster spot for her. Since I couldn't help out with fostering any dogs thanks to Lobo's grumpiness lately, I offered to update her basic vaccinations and run her to the vet for her rabies vaccination that morning before work. Then I would drive her to the kennel to meet Pat who would get her set up for boarding. Quick. Easy. Simple. Unemotional.

"Hi, Bella! Pretty girl! How are you sweet girl?"

"I'm good! This place is nice. My kids aren't here to play with me, but see that couch over there? Yeah, I get to sleep on that, so it's nice."

"I'm glad you're enjoying it here. We'll find you a great forever home with kids to play with and a big comfy couch to sleep on. You just wait. It will be perfect."

"Well, I could just stay here. I mean, there aren't any kids, but there is that couch..."

"Actually, Bella-girl, we're going to get you all up to date on your vaccinations and then you're going to stay at another place for a little while."

"Another place? But, why do I – WHAT is THAT? It looks sharp. What are you doing with that?"

"It won't hurt much, sweetie. Just a quick pinch."

"But. Do I have to? It doesn't look fun. I can't watch." Bella buried her head in Pat's lap and yelped a little when the needle went into her skin, but she sat patiently until I was finished. She didn't even complain when we squirted the Bordatella into her nose. When we were done, she walked willingly with me to the car and hopped in.

"Where are we going, new lady?"

"We just need to make a quick stop at the vet's office so we can make sure you're all healthy. Don't want you getting sick."

"I'm not sick. I'm perfectly healthy."

"Right. And we want to keep you that way."

We pulled into the parking lot, and Bella hopped happily out of the car.

"Do you need to go potty first?"

"Ummmm, yeah, but I'll need you to take this leash off first. I need privacy."

"Well, this is a very busy road. I can't just take the leash off of you. I need to make sure you stay safe."

"Ummmm, ok. But then I can't go potty. I can go smell this spot, though. I know it makes it look like I'm thinking about going potty, but really I'm just smelling stuff. I can't potty with you holding my leash."

"Ok. Let's just go inside, sweet girl."

Bella took one step inside the vet's office and immediately began to whine. I couldn't tell if it was because she had to go potty or because she was afraid of the vet. She wouldn't answer when I asked. She just kept looking around nervously and crying. She cried when we went back to the exam room. She didn't cry when the vet administered the rabies vaccination, but as soon as we walked back out to the waiting area, she began crying again. She walked eagerly through the door as we left and hopped back up into the car and then began worrying again.

"Are we going back to the place with the couch now? It doesn't have kids, but it has a big comfy couch, and the foster lady there is real nice."

"Actually, Bella, we're going to a new place."

"A new place with a couch and kids? Or, at least a couch?"

"It's a nice place. The people there are real nice."

"You're not answering my question."

"AND you'll get to go potty without wearing a leash."

"Ok. What about the couch?"

"You'll have your own room and a door so you can go outside whenever you want."

"My own room with a couch?"

"Pat is bringing you lots of toys and blankets and treats."

"And a couch? Is she bringing me a couch?"

Do you know how difficult it is to lie to a dog that sweet? I mean, the place she was going to was very nice, but it wasn't a home. There was no couch. There were no kids. There might be regular walks and some quick pets, but no long cuddles while watching her favorite show. This girl was such a perfect companion, housetrained, great with kids and other animals, requiring little more than a couch to snuggle on and the occasional run outside. She was a perfect size and had a great temperament. She was a highly adoptable dog, and yet, she was going to a kennel. This is what happens when we run out of foster space. There are simply not enough homes to keep up with the demand, and still dogs and cats are dying in the pound.

We pulled into the kennel, and Bella immediately tucked her tail. When I got out and opened the rear door, she reluctantly stepped out of the car. She didn't say a word as we walked up to the door. She didn't even look up. She just kept her tail tucked and her head bowed as though she was in trouble. When we got to the door, I stopped to assure her that everything would be fine.

"It's because I ran away, isn't it?"

"What? What do you mean?"

"I ran away once at my last home, and now I have to go back to the pound."

"No, sweetie. This isn't the pound. This is just a kennel."

"I didn't run away on purpose. I just saw the door open and wanted to go outside and explore a little bit. I like to explore, but I came right back home. I didn't mean to make anyone mad at me. That's why they sent me back to you, right? So you could bring me here as punishment?"

Her eyes looked so pitiful. She had been rescued from the pound and adopted almost a year before. Her family, with two young children, loved her very much. But sometimes things happen outside of our control. Devastating illness in the family had led them to return this perfect girl to us, and she thought it was her fault. She thought she wasn't good enough.

I knelt down in front of her. "Bella, you listen to me. You are a wonderful, beautiful, perfect, sweet girl. You didn't do anything wrong. You shouldn't have run out of your house and made your family worry, but you're not in trouble. They love you and hated to see you leave, but your momma got very sick and couldn't keep taking care of you. This place is not a pound. I know it's not the same as a real home, but the people here are real nice, and they'll take good care of you until we can find you a new home. A real forever home, this time."

I could tell by her posture that she wasn't convinced, but she quietly said, "Ok" and turned to face the door. We walked in, and Bella kept her head low, refusing to make eye contact with the other animal rescuers standing in the lobby. I handed the kennel worker Bella's paperwork and then knelt down to reassure her more while the others discussed the plan. I whispered calmly in Bella's ear, and I stroked her head, "We have such pretty pictures of you that we already have posted everywhere. Someone is going to see them and fall in love with you. We'll make sure as many people as possible see your picture, and we'll find you the perfect home, Bella. I promise."

She didn't respond. The kennel worker took her leash and walked her quietly back to her kennel. That was the last time I saw Bella. No, nothing tragic. Bella was adopted less than two weeks later by an amazing family that drove three hours to come meet her. They paid more than her adoption fee to cover our costs to board her and took her home where she enjoys a big comfy couch and daily long walks with her adoring mom.

28 BUD

They said his family dumped him at the pound because he had stress-induced seizures. He stopped eating three days ago. He stopped getting up out of his plastic bed three days ago. He stopped hoping for a new home, stopped trying, three days ago. I didn't go to the pound to see him, take his photograph, and tell him it would be ok, that we would find him a family. Someone else did that. I did, however, share his story with someone I thought might be willing to give him a new start, a reason to get up and eat and wag his tail again.

And luckily, I was right. As soon as she agreed to foster him, we pulled Bud out of the pound and took him to meet his new foster mom. He walked right up to her and said, "Hey. It's nice to meet you. Let's go home now."

I watched him walk out the door with her and get into her car. He was confident and content. He was going to be ok. And it wasn't long before he managed to convince his new foster family that he should probably just stay there forever. There was no reason to look for another home. This one was the one he belonged in. Sometimes it's just that easy. If only they all were.

So, the butt on the cover. His name is Jack. You can't see his face, but he is freakin adorable. He had been staying at Bobbi and Steve's, but they needed space for more puppies. So, he came to stay with me, and he was less than thrilled about it.

He was here all of an hour before he got spooked in the yard, wrestled out of his collar, and took off. When people use the term "like a bat outta hell," that's what happened. I chased him around the yard a bit with the sounds of Meatloaf playing in my head. He juked me a few times until I just fell over, and then he took off into the woods.

My neighbors and I spent the next few hours wandering the neighborhood, climbing through the woods, calling for him.

Nothing.

Then more humane society volunteers came out to help. If I hadn't been so distraught over losing a foster dog, I'd have been in awe of how quickly so many people dropped everything and drove to house to help search. But that's what volunteers do. Volunteers are selfless people when it comes to their cause. Volunteers are the people that make the world tolerable.

Still this stubborn little dog refused to make a peep. Eventually his previous foster mom was able to get there to help. She brought his old crate and blankets so we could set them up in the woods in hopes that he would come to the familiar smells when things quieted down.

She stepped out of her vehicle and started talking to us about a plan. Within seconds, a cute little tan dog popped his head out from behind a tree.

"Mama?"

"Jack Jack? Jack Jack!"

That little boy ran full boat towards Bobbi like all was right with the world again.

Bobbi scooped him up and carried him back to my house with a parade of relieved rescue volunteers following.

Over the next few weeks, Jack eventually came to trust me, and he quickly became the house favorite among the masses of young men that resided in my basement on any given day. (I'm talking about my kids, my son and his friends. I'm not, like, running some kind of questionable basement bathhouse or something.)

Jack was in his glory when the boys were home. He would hang out with them excitedly bonding, just one of the guys. When they weren't home, he resigned himself to hanging out with me, and he spent a lot of that time pouting because I was often working.

He just wanted to play and cuddle ALL OF THE TIME. When I was busy studying or working, he would pout in the most adorable ways possible.

Not now, Jack. I'm working.

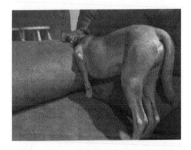

Seriously, Jack Jack. I just need to finish this work.

Stop being so dramatic!

Until finally I put down my work and shifted over so he could squeeze in between my legs and the couch.

He really fit in so well in my home. I just knew I couldn't take on one more animal, and it's not even just about the chaos that having yet one more pet to care for involves. You really have to consider the long-term implications. The cost of caring for one pet can be expensive. Vet visits. Vaccinations. Flea and tick meds. Heartworm meds. Food costs.

But it broke my heart to think of him leaving.

Then one of Trey's friends, one of my kids, one of my favorite kids, decided that Jack was the best friend he'd been waiting for, and I was able to sleep at night knowing that Jack was going to live, just up the road, with someone that he already knew and loved and who would take care of him the rest of his life. That was one of those perfect adoptions that you always hope for, but rarely get to experience.

Why can't they all be happy stories like this?

30 FOR FRANKIE

I'm filled with mixed emotions right now. I am still mourning the loss of Frankie, a sweet, big head of a dog who melted into my hand when I scratched his ear, gave kisses freely, and said more with his soulful eyes than most people can with an entire arsenal of words. What he had to say was powerful, not filled with the empty promises we so often offer to one another. He offered the very real promise of unconditional and lasting love to whoever might save his life. His eyes also said he knew that person would not find him in time ... and that he forgave us for our inability to save him.

Frankie is one of the precious lives that we couldn't save. There just never seems to be enough room. Enough money. Enough time. There are so many that we have no place for. No resources for. No hope for…

And it's so much harder for the ones labeled Pit Bull or Hound. They aren't special enough. Cute enough. Chihuahuas. Puggles.

These are the dogs people want. These are the dogs that will be rescued simply because of their breed.

But not Frankie. Frankie was a Pit Bull. A big, easy going, desperately affectionate Pit Bull. When I would visit him at the pound, he would press his big head into my hand as I scratched his ear, whispering how much I loved him. He accepted that love eagerly, but resignedly. He would listen without judgement as I told him how sorry I was that I didn't have space for him. That I couldn't find someone to take him. Maybe tomorrow. Maybe tomorrow someone would step up. And he let me say those things. But he knew. He knew that no one would be there tomorrow.

And eventually, neither would he.

And then he wasn't.

You can see, then, why I had to write this book. Why I had to share at least some of their stories. Why I am filled with a mix of regret and hope. Regret for not saving Frankie or Buster's brother or any of the pound cats or countless others.

But also hope that someday soon we can save them all.

These are the stories of only a few of the animals that have walked through my life over the last several years. There are so many more that I've had the honor to care for, even for just a short time. There are significantly more that are still out there needing our help. They're sitting in cold, lonely animal shelters. They are chained to a tree. They are dumped on the side of the road. They are living off of dumpster scraps.

I urge you to reach out to your local animal rescue organization and find out how you can help. Volunteer. Foster. Donate. Share the stories of animals in their care. Encourage your friends to adopt rather than buying from pet stores or unregistered backyard breeders. There is always a way to help.

Below are the organizations that I know and trust and that I know would put any donation or support you can offer to good use.

Bedford Humane Society

829 Ole Turnpike Dr, Bedford, VA 24523

All American Mutt Rescue

5491 Johnson Mountain Rd, Huddleston, VA 24104

Angels of Assisi

415 Campbell Ave SW, Roanoke, VA 24016

Made in the USA
Columbia, SC
25 February 2020